THE
Flannery O'Connor
COMPANION

Flannery O'Connor. Photograph by Ralph Morrissey, courtesy of Mrs. Eleanor F. Morrissey and Special Collections, Vanderbilt University Library, Nashville, Tennessee.

THE
Flannery O'Connor
COMPANION

JAMES A. GRIMSHAW, JR.

GREENWOOD PRESS
WESTPORT, CONNECTICUT • LONDON, ENGLAND

Library of Congress Cataloging in Publication Data

Grimshaw, James A
  The Flannery O'Connor companion.

  Bibliography: p.
  Includes index.
  1.   O'Connor, Flannery—Criticism and interpretation.
I.   Title.
PS3565.C57Z68   813'.54   80-26828
ISBN 0-313-21086-1 (lib. bdg.)

Library of Congress Catalog Card Number: 80-26828
ISBN: 0-313-21086-1

First published in 1981

Greenwood Press
a division of Congressional Information Service, Inc.
88 Post Road West, Westport, Connecticut 06881

Printed in the United States of America

10 9 8 7 6 5 4 3 2 1

To
Joe and Jean Tuso

. . . for the one thing that man fears
Is the terror of salvation and the face
Of glory. . . .

—Robert Penn Warren
BROTHER TO DRAGONS
A Tale In Verse and Voices
(A New Version)

Contents

Illustrations

Preface

The Flannery O'Connor Companion introduces readers to the writings—nonfiction, fiction, and letters—of Mary Flannery O'Connor (1925-1964), a Southern, Catholic writer who died young, age thirty-nine, of lupus. As an introduction it considers among its audience first-time readers of O'Connor, some of whom may be students exposed to only one story in a survey class or pupils studying her essays in a creative writing course. Others may be avid readers exploring "new" writers, or Christians seeking a better understanding of their religion.

Also, among this volume's considered audience are those who have read, studied, and perhaps taught O'Connor's works previously and who will find some suggestions—via approaches and associations—heretofore undeveloped among the vast amounts of criticism available. Thus, *The Flannery O'Connor Companion* will fulfill its second purpose as convenient reference guide with notes and a selected bibliography.

There is yet another audience: the visual group that comes to O'Connor's works through films. *The Displaced Person* has been aired on public television, and with a limited release is John Huston's production of *Wise Blood*. *Good Country People* and *The Life You Save May Be Your Own* have also been filmed, and a number of documentaries include references or background to O'Connor's "world," one of the latest of which is *Let the Spirit Move*, about a street preacher in Atlanta. *The Flannery O'Connor Companion* should serve those audiences as well.

The organization offers a straightforward approach to O'Connor's works. The introduction in the first chapter gathers some broad points about her writing, points which my students in Colorado and in Georgia have raised over the years. Some of the questions about the readings are introduced in this first chapter; the "answers" follow in succeeding chapters. Discussions of her essays and stories are arranged, for convenience, in the order that the works appear in *Mystery and Manners* and *The Complete Stories*, respectively.

Chapter 4 catalogues O'Connor's fictional characters, a catalogue not published before, to the best of my knowledge. Its being follows an already established precedent in the Greenwood Press companion series and for other authors in other series as well: *Who's Who in Faulkner* and "A Character Index of Robert Penn Warren's Long Works of Fiction" (*Emporia State Research Studies*), for example. The utility of such a listing needs neither further explanation nor justification.

"O'Connor's Place in Twentieth-Century Literature" relates the three primary areas in which readers encounter her works: in regional literature of the South, in religious literature among Roman Catholics, and in women's literature. Those areas are not mutually exclusive, however; and O'Connor's fiction indeed transcends each of them as art. Her "habit of art" is to be taken as a whole, unified and complete. But teachers and critics continue to categorize her work, and the fifth chapter examines those categories.

The two appendices serve different purposes. The first briefly describes selected Catholic and other Christian existentialist influences on O'Connor. It provides sources for further study of those influences and suggests the ideas and beliefs that O'Connor either incorporated or opposed in her fiction. Some of the opposite views are included because they seem to have been as stimulating to her imagination as similar beliefs upon which her most fervent convictions and faith rested. The second appendix reproduces her "Introduction to *A Memoir of Mary Ann*," as poignant a disclosure of O'Connor's own personality as it is of Mary Ann's charity. It is, in my opinion, one of Flannery O'Connor's most artistic pieces.

I am reminded of two quotations that capture what I would like to believe this volume brings to light for O'Connor's audiences. One is from Robert Penn Warren's essay, "Why Do We Read Fiction?": "Why do we read fiction? The answer is simple. We read it because we like it. And we like it because fiction, as an image of life, stimulates and gratifies our interest in life."[1] The second is from John Gardner's essay *On Moral Fiction*: "We study people . . . in order to understand them and fully experience our exchange with them . . . [which] can contribute to art and is natural to art, since the soul of art is celebration and discovery through imitation."[2] O'Connor's writings reflect her interest in life. They represent her celebration of life. In those terms, she blossoms as Mary Ann does, another flower on that same tree.

J. A. G., Jr.

Acknowledgments

I am indebted to the following individuals and institutions for their valuable help, suggestions, and encouragement in the preparation of this book:

Professor Joseph F. Tuso, former Head, Department of English, Georgia College, and now Head, Department of English, New Mexico State University, who provided the initial opportunity for me to work in the O'Connor Collection; and Mary Barbara Tate and James O. Tate, both of whom shared delightful evenings of conversation about Flannery O'Connor. William C. Simpson, Dean, School of Arts and Sciences, Georgia College, for the appointment as Flannery O'Connor Visiting Professor.

Charles E. Beard, Director of Libraries, and Gerald Becham, Curator of the O'Connor Collection, Georgia College, for the many courtesies rendered during my stay.

Brainard Cheney and Andrew Lytle, for permission to examine their correspondence with Flannery O'Connor, on file in the Vanderbilt University Library; Ms. Marice Wolfe, Head of Special Collections, Vanderbilt University Library, and her staff for making my work there go smoothly; and Mrs. Eleanor F. Morrissey for permission to use the photograph of Flannery O'Connor, taken by her late husband, Mr. Ralph Morrissey.

William J. Marshall, Head of Special Collections and Archives, University of Kentucky Libraries, for sharing his catalogue of the Thomas Merton papers on file there.

The interlibrary loan staff, United States Air Force Academy, for prompt, courteous service over the years.

Colonel Jack M. Shuttleworth, Head, Department of English, United States Air Force Academy, for providing the time to complete this project; C. Hugh Holman, Kenan Professor of English, University of North Carolina at Chapel Hill, for illuminating comments about Flannery O'Connor; and Lewis P. Simpson, Boyd Professor of English, Louisiana State University at Baton Rouge, for continued guidance and support.

Brigadier General Jesse C. Gatlin, Jr. (USAF, Ret.), and Major William E. McCarron, Associate Professor of English, United States Air Force Academy, for critical readings of this volume in earlier drafts.

John Hazard Wildman, Louisiana State University, and Alfred M. Kern, Allegheny College, Pennsylvania, for their wise counsel; H. F. Lippincott, Montgomery, Alabama, for bibliographical assistance; and Stuart B. James, Denver University, for use of his copy of Flannery O'Connor's master's thesis.

The Reverend Stanley G. MacGirvin, Saint Athanasius Anglican Catholic Church, Colorado Springs, for his lively sermons and theological discussions.

My English 444/544 students at Georgia College: Norma Andrews, Michael H. Blatt, Michael B. Boling, Thomas E. Brannen, Jr., Willene R. Burney, Marie L. Crider, Shirley J. Farrell, Charles S. Ford, Hester S. Fults, Hope P. Payne, John M. Sirmans, Betty L. Stansberry, Doris S. Taylor, and Joan A. White—from whom I learned a great deal.

Dode Jones for typing final copy.

And my wife, Darlene, and children, Courtney and James, for their continued patience.

The success of this volume is due in large part to them; its shortcomings are mine alone.

Abbreviations

THE
Flannery O'Connor
COMPANION

1

Introduction: On Reading Flannery O'Connor

Readers of Flannery O'Connor's works often find themselves beset with subject matter that only appears to be familiar to them. Or they are perplexed by strange reversals of characters, the "good guys" frequently holding the short end of the stick and coming off as "bad guys." Or they sense religious implications in the stories, but they are not quite sure about the religion. Or they wonder bemusedly about the place O'Connor has chosen to write about. Reactions to one and all of those "obstacles" vary only in degree: from mild skepticism to bold accusations of absurdity.

Yet the critical attention scholars, students, and readers have paid O'Connor suggests that there is something in her fiction worth the ferreting, worth the second look, even worth some introspection. Much of that critical attention has, in the past, dwelt on particular biographical facts about her life: she suffered early from a disease which had already claimed her father and which would surely cut short her life[1]; she was a devout Roman Catholic, devoted to carrying the Word to all her readers; she was a Southerner with all that being southern implies about a "distorted" view of life. Of the various approaches employed to explain O'Connor's fiction, the one which has drawn the most attention and offered the most convenient "answers" has been the religious system. This explanation is certainly not without just cause. A knowledge of Roman Catholicism, as well as existentialism and Protestantism, will enrich readers' enjoyment of her stories. That "special" knowledge is not necessary, however, to have the stories fulfill their dual purpose: to entertain and to instruct.

Some critics of O'Connor's works have questioned the entertainment value of stories that deal with "freaks" such as Rufus Johnson in "The Lame Shall Enter First" and with violence such as mass murder in "A Good Man Is Hard To Find." But those commentators apparently have short memories in recalling what constitutes entertainment. The Greeks, for example, revered Hephaestus, god of fire and metalworking, although he was lame; and certainly what could be more violent than Oedipus' killing his father, causing the death of his mother, and gouging his own eyes out. The entertainment value does not lie in the violence per se, but in the interaction of people caught in the inextricable web of the human condition, people who, like their audiences everywhere, struggle to find meaning in their lives. Something that entertains (*tenēre* = to hold) engages its audience; O'Connor's fiction does that.

Humor, a term commonly associated with entertainment, is another aspect that O'Connor combines effectively with violence. The technique is not new. When O'Connor has the Misfit say about the Grandmother, "She would of been a good woman if it had been somebody there to shoot her every minute of her life,"[2] we smile at least momentarily at the simplicity of truth in the statement, though O'Connor's message is serious.

Instruction thus links with entertainment. That so many writers concatenate these two purposes also bothers readers. How engaging would literature (or other art forms as well) be without instruction? Consider movies, for example. A recent winner of four academy awards, *All That Jazz*, portrays a dying man's thoughts. The film is specifically about death. Entertaining? Apparently moviegoers found it so. Instructive? Perhaps that, too. O'Connor finds that subject worthy of her attention; it is, after all, the end of man and a topic engaging man's thoughts time out of mind.[3] When writers address such a serious subject, they have basically two approaches from which to choose: a nonreligious view or a religious one. The film mentioned above takes the former approach; O'Connor, the latter. Both are instructive and indeed can complement the other. What is it like to view death from a secular point of view? For Joe Gideon, it is a dance routine in *All That Jazz*, the summation of one's life. From a religious point of view? A vision of gaunt trees in mysterious dark files marching across the water for the grandfather in "A View of the Woods," another symbolic summation of one's life.

Such entertainment and instruction leave readers in different emotional states of mind, depending largely on what they bring with them to the films and stories. Nonreligious readers may despair over what seems to them incomplete endings, unresolved conflicts, and gratuitous violence. Believers, on the other hand, may read sometimes in stark terror and at other times in grateful recognition of the unusual and unexpected ways in which God bestows Grace. For the latter group of readers, her stories offer optimism and hope, hope for some of her characters as well as hope in their lives. O'Connor's brand of entertainment recalls a line from Shakespeare's *Merry Wives of Windsor*: "I thinke the best way were, to entertaine him with hope" (II.i.68). That view—optimistic and instilled with hope—is one of the premises of this book, one of the guides for reading O'Connor.

The four points mentioned in the opening paragraph of this introduction—subject, characters, religion, and place—are topics of the general remarks that follow and of the specific chapters which constitute the remainder of this book. They are not all that can be said; readers may consult the works cited in the notes and selected bibliography for more detailed discussions. Rather, these remarks should serve merely as convenient companions in exploring the world of Flannery O'Connor.

SUBJECT MATTER

Robert Penn Warren has said in interviews that every writer has but one story to tell and the good writers have more versions of their story.[4] That is true of O'Connor; and if it is true that poet Donald Justice's central theme can be identified as "loss,"[5] then O'Connor's might be said to be "gain," or the possibility of gain. Actually, one implies the other. The gain at which O'Connor's characters have a chance is spiritual gain through self-knowledge and revelation; and spiritual gain is contingent on proffered Grace, acceptance of which is one of two possibilities.

In a 14 April 1960 letter to John Hawkes, O'Connor explains the difficult term "Grace" this way:

Grace, to the Catholic way of thinking, can and does use as its medium the imperfect, purely human, and even hypocritical. Cutting yourself off from Grace is a very decided matter, requiring a real choice, act of will, and affecting the very ground of the soul. The Misfit is touched by the Grace that comes through the old lady [the Grandmother] when she recognizes him as her child, as she has been touched by the Grace that comes through him in his particular suffering (*HB*, p. 389).

O'Connor sees the Grace working in the Misfit, too; and although the Grandmother loses her life, she has gained that inward moment which may be offered at any time but is not always accepted.

O'Connor's stories are replete with those moments: Mrs. May in "Greenleaf" seems to receive such an offer just before the loose bull gores her; Mrs. Cope in "A Circle in the Fire" as she watches the fire in her meadow; and Tarwater in *The Violent Bear It Away* after his degradation. The instruments that deliver those moments are varied and usually unexpected. The bull in the pasture gores Mrs. May; three unmannerly, unruly boys set fire to Mrs. Cope's field; and a homosexual rapes Tarwater. What readers notice and are shocked about in each of these moments, and others in other stories, is the grotesqueness and physical violence involved.

The grotesque and violence in fiction have been subjects of many discussions, and literature abounds with examples of each. In fact, Hemingway in *The Sun Also Rises* uses a bull to end the love affair of Lady Brett Ashley and the bullfighter Pedro Romero, and Hemingway gives Jake Barnes a war wound which deprives him of loving Brett. In Graham Greene's story "The Destructors" a gang of juvenile delinquents demolish "Old Misery's" beautiful, old house for no apparent reason. In James Dickey's novel *Deliverance*, one of the fishermen is brutally raped in an explicit scene of sodomy. We notice, however, that not even in Greene's story does Grace abound. But in O'Connor's work, it does. The point, not farfetched, is this: Hemingway's writing draws from the existentialists' philosophy of the absurdity of existence, a stance not unknown to O'Connor and therefore to some of her characters; Greene belongs to that group of writers labeled, sometimes misleadingly, "Catholic writers"; and Dickey's only novel is characteristically Southern. Thus, grotesqueness and violence do not necessarily lead inevitably to an opportunity for revelation and Grace, but do so frequently in O'Connor's works. We are prepared for Mrs. May's fate when she impatiently honks her car horn, a sound Mr. Greenleaf has told her irritates that particular bull. Mrs. Cope's fear of fire on her property and the attitude of the three "visitors" to her farm alert us to the inevitable consequence, fire. Tarwater's encounters with the devil become progressively more violent; his final encounter culminates in the devil's ultimate violation of his body. All three grotesque acts jar our sensibilities and awaken us to the transformation of each character. They become decision points for those characters.

Each one, nonetheless, is free to choose, free to accept or reject Grace. Mrs. May's decision must be final in her death. Mrs. Cope, on the other hand, is left to make her decision. O'Connor's clue, which does not resolve for the reader what Mrs. Cope decides, is the look of misery upon her face at the end of the story. Tarwater's decision is so pronounced as to appear almost didactic as he sets his face "toward the dark city where the children of God lay sleeping" (*VBIA*, p. 243). O'Connor leaves her characters to decide of their own free will and according to her development of them. She does not deceive her audience.

Because she is an artist first, O'Connor never "cheats."[6] She leads her readers with her characters to those moments of decision. Yet her readers often recoil with revulsion because they, too, seem to be confronted with the same choice. To accept or not to accept becomes the question. Artistically we must applaud the skill with which she renders the stories.

Morally and theologically we are on our own to contemplate the mystery of our existence.[7] If we do contemplate that mystery as O'Connor presents it, we arrive at a moment of decision, too; and if we accept what is proffered, O'Connor then achieves what Tolstoy has called the highest purpose of art: "to make people good by choice."[8]

The identification of O'Connor's central theme, her subject matter, as the possibility of gain implies more than it states. Gardner's claim that "great art celebrates life's potential, offering a vision unmistakably and unsentimentally rooted in love"[9] pertains unequivocally to O'Connor's subject. Her characters all stand to gain love, a divine love (*agapē*) bestowed through Grace. Other forms of love also manifest themselves in varying degrees: lust or passion, such as the seduction of Hulga by the Bible salesman in "Good Country People"; friendship or love of one's neighbor as in Mrs. Connin's concern for Harry Ashfield in "The River"; narcissistic love personified in Asbury Fox in "The Enduring Chill" and Mrs. Turpin in "Revelation"; marital love in "Parker's Back"; and familial love which next to *agapē* predominates O'Connor's concern.

Familial love pervades most of O'Connor's stories in a negative way. That is, the absence of familial love or familial love misdirected focuses our attention on the shortcomings of her main characters. In "The Geranium" Old Dudley's daughter's feeling of obligation toward her father suggests her own selfishness and precipitates the action. Julian's feelings of hostility center on his mother's concern for her family's bloodlines in "Everything That Rises Must Converge." Mr. Fortune's pride in Mary Fortune, his granddaughter in "A View of the Woods," climaxes in a misguided and mistaken love. The absence of real love allows O'Connor to develop her theme of possibility of gain since reconciliation itself suggests gain. When the characters put aside selfish desires in order to help a member of the family, they clear away the obstacles that would also deny them *agapē*. Julian, for example, shows unselfish and genuine concern for his mother only after she has had an unpleasant encounter followed by a stroke. Ironically his concern protects him momentarily from entering "the world of guilt and sorrow" (*CS*, p. 420).

O'CONNOR'S CHARACTERS

To separate subject and characters is at best an artificial approach, and we must take seriously O'Connor's following statement: "In the act of writing, one sees that the way a thing is made controls and is inseparable from the whole meaning of it" (*MM*, p. 129). Since her stories are built around people, an understanding of them leads to our better understanding of her subject. Again Gardner's essay makes the point: "We study people carefully for two main reasons: in order to understand them and fully experience our exchange with them, or in order to feel ourselves superior."[10] The second reason Gardner dismisses as petty. Unfortunately, too many readers of O'Connor's fiction find the second reason more suitable to their liking. How easy it is for us to feel superior to the hypocrites, the bigots, the zealots who parade across O'Connor's pages. To stop at that, however, disallows us to understand them and O'Connor. To do so unwittingly gives witness to her belief "that the basic experience of everyone is the experience of human limitation" (*MM*, p. 131). Consequently, when O'Connor writes of human limitation, some of her characters' limitations are physical. Those characters have become known as O'Connor's "freaks."

But O'Connor is not maligning the physically and mentally handicapped. She is dramatizing in their outward and tangible forms human limitations. The truly handicapped and crippled are usually those characters who do not recognize their own flaws and limitations, flaws that in Greek drama become tragic flaws and lead to the possessors' downfall and calamity. In her essay "The Teaching of Literature," O'Connor addresses the discomfort her readers feel when they read about "freaks": "The freak in modern fiction is usually disturbing to us because he keeps us from forgetting that we share his state" (*MM*, p. 133). If artists present their freaks as *complete* persons, then O'Connor says we should feel uneasy. O'Connor's characters are not complete persons; they lack compassion, love, confidence, self-knowledge—at least one of the attributes which would enable them to be whole. That Rufus Johnson has a club foot or that Hulga has a wooden leg, per se, is not the point at all. In fact, O'Connor uses those physical limitations as symbols of bigger limitations—Rufus's meanness, Sheppard's club soul, Hulga's wooden soul.

O'Connor reveals her incomplete characters through manners, that is, through the customs, conventions, and convictions of their society. Most of her characters are the poor, because they "only symbolize for [the writer] the state of all men" (*MM*, p. 132). Their customs are more natural, less clouded by facades, their conventions are ritualistic and reflect more openly the basic needs of man, and their convictions—whether we agree or disagree—are not obscured by ambiguities. They say what they mean and mean what they say. Their speech is colorful and provides the metaphors necessary for their identity. Nor do they underestimate man's capacity for error. Juxtaposed to them are the once-wealthy and well-to-do who still cling to their pasts. This dichotomy among her characters enables O'Connor to build tensions which lead the characters on to their "moments." In drama, such opposites are called foils: Mrs. Pritchard against Mrs. Cope in "A Circle in the Fire"; Mrs. Shortley and Mrs. McIntyre in "The Displaced Person"; Mrs. Freeman and Mrs. Hopewell in "Good Country People"; and

Mrs. Greenleaf versus Mrs. May in "Greenleaf," come immediately to mind.

To recognize human limitations is one feat; to admit they exist is entirely another; but to choose to correct them is perhaps the greatest accomplishment. We acknowledge that O'Connor as artist has done all three; her characters have not, and that is where their struggle comes in. Rather, our struggle, because as readers we too have difficulty admitting that those limitations are common to all men. In almost formulaic fashion, O'Connor's "good guys" turn out to be the not-so-good, to be people we recognize and in whom we recognize a part of ourselves. Remember Archie Bunker on the television series *All in the Family*? O'Connor's stories are full of Archie Bunkers. Unlike the script writers for that program, though, O'Connor forces her characters to recognize their foibles and to grapple with their biases. Instead of ending with a laugh, O'Connor's stories end with a frown, if not a tear. Once the characters recover from the shock of recognition, if they do, and admit their limitations, they have an alternative: to ignore them or to try to correct them.

Ignoring limitations can be fatal, or if not fatal at least self-condemning. Hazel Motes, the main character in *Wise Blood*, tries to turn his back on his "calling" to be a man of God. His inward struggle becomes the motivating force which leads him to found the Church Without Christ, to lead a shiftless life of sin, including murder and fornication, and finally to blind himself. In "The Barber," an early story, Rayber ignores the limits of the culture in which he lives and tries to "educate" some of the townspeople, an attempt which results in his own humiliation and disgrace. Asbury Fox in "The Enduring Chill" ignores simple precautions while working in his mother's dairy to the detriment of his physical and subsequent spiritual well-being. All three lack compassion, love, and self-knowledge and resist their opportunities for gaining them.

Correcting limitation, on the other hand, can be equally difficult. Surely the struggle is as fierce within, and over, the individual. When Tarwater finally performs the sacrament of baptism on Bishop in *The Violent Bear It Away*, he begins to combat the limitations his great-uncle has seemingly placed on him and which his uncle tries to undo. The child Harry Ashfield in "The River" overcomes the source of his limitations, his indifferent parents, by baptizing himself again and seeking the Kingdom of Christ in the river. The child in "A Temple of the Holy Ghost," once arrogant and quick to judge others, recognizes most explicitly of all O'Connor's characters the moment of illumination during a celebration of the Holy Eucharist.

Too much generalizing about O'Connor's characters would do a disservice to O'Connor as an artist, but certain "types" do recur often enough to deserve mention: pseudointellectuals, hypocrites and great pretenders, and recalcitrant children.

Pseudointellectuals include those with formal education but without knowledge. This formidable group is large: Rayber ("The Barber"), Hulga ("Good Country People"), Asbury ("The Enduring Chill"), Julian ("Everything That Rises Must Converge"), Calhoun and Mary Elizabeth ("The Partridge Festival"), and Rayber (*VBIA*). O'Connor is quick to point out through such examples the sin of Pride as a direct descendant of man's fall from Grace in the Garden. Their "education" stands in their way of knowing, and they become exhibits against our modern educational system, a subject O'Connor explores in her essay, "Total Effect and the Eighth Grade." It is not that O'Connor is anti-intellectual, I think, but rather she is concerned about the deeper problem of intellectualism replacing religion, becoming a religion for some. Hulga's belief in nothing, for example, sprouts from her reading of the early twentieth-century existentialist, Martin Heidegger. A portion of his essay "What Is Metaphysics?" has been marked by Hulga and is read at random by her mother who finds the passage "like some evil incantation in gibberish" (*CS*, p. 277).[11] For Hulga, it has become an obstacle rather than a passageway to deeper understanding and belief.[12]

The list of hypocrites and great pretenders is perhaps longer than the list of pseudointellectuals. Without being exhaustive, the following come to mind: Miss Willerton ("The Crop"), Lucynell Crater ("The Life You Save May Be Your Own"), Mrs. Cope ("A Circle in the Fire"), Mrs. McIntyre ("The Displaced Person"), Mr. Head ("The Artificial Nigger"), Mrs. May ("Greenleaf"), and Mrs. Turpin ("Revelation"). The hypocrites savor for the most part a feeling of superiority and self-righteousness about their superiority. Mrs. Turpin will serve as the paradigm for this illustration. Sometimes suffering from insomnia, she mulls over the question of who "she would have chosen to be if she couldn't have been herself" (*CS*, p. 491). She imagines that Jesus, Himself, gives her the choice between being "a nigger or white-trash," a choice she is hard pressed to make: " 'All right, make me a nigger then—but that don't mean a trashy one.' And he would have made her a neat clean respectable Negro woman, herself but black" (*CS*, p. 491). The great pretenders, such as Mrs. May, live out their lives in what-might-have-been. Mrs. May's two sons are worthless, lazy, disrespectful children-grown-adults. She pretends, however, that they are up-and-coming young men and is constantly comparing them to the Greenleaf boys, who in contrast are up-and-coming. O'Connor here seems most blatant in portraying individuals who are blind to their own limitations and shortcomings. Some receive a jolt which alters their self-awarensss (Mrs. Turpin); a few do not.

A third category of O'Connor's characters includes recalcitrant children who seem to go out of their way to make themselves despicable: John Wesley and June Star ("A Good Man Is Hard To Find"), John Wesley Poker Sash ("A Late Encounter with the Enemy"), the three boys ("A Circle in the Fire"), the child before her moment of Grace ("A Temple of the Holy Ghost"), Nelson ("The Artificial Nigger"), Mary Fortune Pitts ("A View of the Woods")—the list seems endless. Why children, readers ask? Children without proper guidance might be the response. If people suffer the little children and bring them to Christ, O'Connor seems to be saying, then they have a convert for life. Their minds are impressionable. Likewise, if led astray, they are perhaps lost for life. Rayber, Tarwater's uncle in *VBIA*, has the fanatical belief that old Tarwater warped him and his great-nephew. Sheppard in "The Lame Shall Enter First" becomes so engrossed in "saving" Rufus Johnson, a juvenile delinquent, that he ignores his own son, Norton. The effects are dramatic and shocking: Tarwater drowns Bishop, the mongoloid son of Rayber, and Rufus leads Norton to suicide. Perhaps O'Connor has a second motive for using children so frequently. The mystery of existence entails the mystery of good and evil, both of which are forces in children's as well as adults' lives. What protection, O'Connor may be askng, does a child have against such forces? Baptism at birth. Confirmation, or acceptance, however, comes later—at about the age of her children characters. They, too, are faced with a choice; and their parents must carry the burden of guilt if their children are not prepared for that choice. Mr. Head, for example, agonizes over Nelson's choice to visit the city, a choice for which he has not been adequately prepared. In the penultimate paragraph of that story, O'Connor makes her most explicit statement about this subject: "[Mr. Head] understood that [the action of mercy] grew out of agony, which is not denied to any man and which is given in strange ways to children" (*CS*, p. 269). Mr. Head traces his sins back to the Original Sin and truly realizes his moment of Grace with Nelson's help; Mr. Head is changed by the experience.[13]

RELIGION

In treating subject matter and characterization, we have already touched on this point of religion; but a few additional points remain to be made. Although O'Connor was a Roman Catholic, she seems to treat Protestantism more than she does Catholicism, and some readers wonder why. This impression is erroneous. In one letter to "A" dated 20 July 1955, O'Connor writes:

I think that the Church is the only thing that is going to make the terrible world we are coming to endurable; the only thing that makes the Church endurable is that it is somehow the body of Christ and that on this we are fed. It seems to be a fact that you have to suffer as much from the Church as for it but if you believe in the divinity of Christ, you have to cherish the world at the same time that you struggle to endure it (*HB*, p. 90).

Often her Protestant characters find the world unbearable because they lack that belief, that understanding which has as its basis Catholic dogma. That dogma, O'Connor contends, is "a gateway to contemplation and is an instrument of freedom and not of restriction" (*HB*, p. 92).

In his book *The Religions of Man*, Huston Smith considers the "two most important concepts for the understanding of [the Catholic] institution: the Church as Teaching Authority, and the Church as Sacramental Agent."[14] O'Connor was reared a Catholic, went to Catholic schools, and remained a devout Catholic throughout her thirty-nine years (*HB*, p. 114). The Church as Teaching Authority, that is, the doctrine of papal infallibility, went without question. The use of the sacraments in her fiction also was unquestioned but has a greater influence on her fiction. Either directly or indirectly, all seven are there: Baptism, Confirmation, Holy Matrimony, Holy Orders, Extreme Unction, Confession, and Holy Eucharist. About her use of baptism, she makes this comment in her essay "Novelist and Believer": "When I write a novel [*VBIA*] in which the central action is a baptism, I am very well aware that for a majority of my readers, baptism is a meaningless rite, and so in my novel I have to see that this baptism carries enough awe and mystery to jar the reader in to some kind of emotional recognition of its significance" (*MM*, p. 162). Even some of her Catholic critics missed her intention, and for most of her life her works were not well-received by the Catholic press.

Simply the fact that she was a Catholic and a writer did not put her at odds with all Protestantism. Smith cites the "two most distinctive features [of Protestantism], namely Justification by Faith, and the Protestant Principle."[15] The Justification by Faith includes a movement of total self toward God, a preparation for the bestowal of Grace, although O'Connor notes that Grace comes unexpectedly and in surprising ways. Surely it does not distinguish among religious affiliations, but she writes to "A" on 15 September 1955:

Also I don't think . . . that to be a true Christian you believe that mutual interdependence is a conceit. That is far from Catholic doctrine; in fact it strikes me as highly Protestant, a sort of justification by faith. God becomes not only a man, but Man. This is the mystery of the Redemption and our salvation is worked out on earth according as we love one another, see Christ in one another, etc., by works (*HB*, p. 102).

Defining the second feature, the Protestant Principle, as a warning against idolatry, we are reminded of Enoch Emery in *Wise Blood* and the Carmody's daughter-evangelist who represents a surrogate idol in *The Violent Bear It Away*. She uses both features to strengthen the Christian belief in Christ.

One additional quotation from O'Connor's letters helps put religion into context in her fiction:

Fiction is the concrete expression of mystery—mystery that is lived. Catholics believe that all creation is good and that evil is the wrong use of good and that without Grace we use it wrong most of the time. It's almost impossible to write about supernatural Grace in fiction. As to natural Grace, we have to take that the way it comes—through nature. In any case, it operates surrounded by evil (*HB*, p. 144).[16]

Both nature and evil are prevalent in her stories. To some of her characters, such as Mr. Fortune in "A View of the Woods," nature is simply nature, there for man's use and exploitation. For others, such as the Pitts family, the woods represent more; their feelings about the woods are almost religious. Evil abounds so much that citing specific examples at this time would be perfunctory. O'Connor believed, though, that her characters (and readers, too) could learn about the devil through their encounters with him; and in fact that they had to encounter evil in order to exercise their freedom of choice between God and the devil.

Although I made the statement at the beginning of this introduction that a "special" knowledge of religions is not necessary to enjoy her fiction—and I still contend that that is so—religion does play an underlying role which when recognized enhances meaning and appreciation. Appendix 1 contains references to some Roman Catholic and Christian existentialist influences for those readers who would like to explore this possibility further.

PLACE

Why does it matter that most of Flannery O'Connor's stories are set in the South—around Milledgeville, Georgia, her hometown for most of her life, to be specific? She wrote about the place she knew; many of her descriptions, especially of the encircling line of trees, can be seen from the front porch of Andalusia, her mother's farm about four miles north of Milledgeville. If her stories were merely regional, merely about a condition of people peculiar only to that region, place would have more importance. Like Faulkner's Yoknapatawpha county in Mississippi, O'Connor's little corner of the world is simply setting, a vehicle for her concerns about a larger concern.

*Andalusia Farm, four miles north of Milledgeville,
Georgia. Photograph by the author.*

The South does, however, provide an atmosphere conducive to those concerns. The South is a sensuous region, that is, a region which makes constant demands on its inhabitants' senses. That may be one reason so many "Southern" writers make use of sights, sounds, and smells in their fiction. Travelers through middle Georgia in mid-July can comprehend this sensuousness immediately: they see the densely grown, vine-covered trees on both sides of the two-lane farm-to-market road as they chase heat waves emanating from the pavement; they hear the insects, the birds, the squeal of hot rubber on asphalt—sounds of heat; they smell the fecund earth, the heavy sweetness of honeysuckle and pine in a closeness that almost stiffles breath; they taste the humidity; and they feel it. Too, they sense the omnipotent oppressiveness of a world encased within itself, allowing freedom of movement within but making escape seem impossible. O'Connor's fiction is full of descriptions of nature in this world.

Climate alone does not create a sense of place. It requires people who share common interests, common bonds, and a sense of community.[17] Southerners. Outsiders first recognize them by their manner of speech, their dialect.[18] The better southern writers have an ear for that dialect and they use it. A story may illustrate this sensitivity. When the director and script writers for the film *The Displaced Person* tried to change the dialogue, they found that the story just "did not come off." Only by reverting to O'Connor's dialogue in her story did they achieve the proper effect in the film. The film version of "The Life You Save May Be Your Own" also follows closely O'Connor's dialogue. O'Connor's letter to Cecil Dawkins, dated 20 September 1958, underscores the need to get the speech right in southern stories. Among other points which she makes on this topic, O'Connor suggests that the word "kid" would be inappropriate as Dawkins uses it in the story "Hummers in the Larkspur" (*HB*, p. 296). O'Connor's ear is particularly tuned to the rhythm of speech in middle Georgia: pronunciation ("bidnis"), syntax, and diction.

Strangers to the South might next notice the manners. Southerners tend to pay attention to formalities and social amenities that in other parts of the country have ceased to or never did exist. To outside observers, those formalities suggest a falseness, an aura of pseudosophistication. The greeting even to strangers on the street, the use of "Yes Mam" and "No Sir" to one's elders, the role of women in society, the attention to the best for guests—all of those examples are small manifestations of what Al Kern has called "the hum and buzz of culture."[19] In some instances, manners form a polite facade behind which southerners can scrutinize others; in other instances, manners provide guidelines, rules of conduct for people who are civilized and who want to be treated civilly. They are taught at home through tradition and mutual acceptance and without proclamation.[20] O'Connor notes that "the

"Tilman operated a combination country store, filling station, scrap-metal dump, used-car lot and dance hall. . . ." ("A View of the Woods") Photograph by Barbara McKenzie, reprinted by permission of Barbara McKenzie and The Georgia Review.

South has survived in the past because its manners, however lopsided or inadequate they may have been, provided enough social discipline to hold us together and give us an identity" (*MM*, p. 234).

That identity, or sense of community as it has come to be known, is more than mere regional pride. It was present before 1861, but the Civil War brought it to the forefront and helped give it definition. As ironic as it may sound to some, that identity is based in a sense of values of the worth of the individual. When that value is forgotten, calamitous results occur. The characters live in what Robert Penn Warren has called in *All the King's Men* the "agony of will," a concept which Jack Burden, the protagonist in the novel, comes to live with in these terms: ". . . a man's virtue may be but the defect of his desire, as his crime may be but a function of his virtue."[21] O'Connor might reply, yes, "what has given the South her identity are . . . a distrust of the abstract, a sense of human dependence on the grace of God, and *a knowledge that evil is not simply a problem to be solved, but a mystery to be endured*" (*MM*, p. 209; italics added) individually and collectively. In southern literature, Lewis P. Simpson says in his essay, "The Southern Novelist and Southern Nationalism," writers have represented their literary construction of human existence in the South "as a quest for a revelation of man's moral community in history."[22] O'Connor's quest begins at the beginning for Christians.

Each of the four topics broached above—subject matter, characterization, religion, and place—is too large for complete coverage here. Their introduction, however, gives an overview of this book and its remaining chapters and offers for those who must read and run, thoughts to ponder as they approach O'Connor's fiction.

Cline House in Milledgeville, Georgia, Flannery's home as a girl and still her mother's (Mrs. Regina Cline O'Connor's) home. Photograph by Barbara McKenzie, reprinted by permission of Barbara McKenzie and The Georgia Review.

2

The Nonfiction

O'Connor's essays discuss, in part, the art (mystery) of her stories and the craft (form) of her writing; and her stories illustrate many of the theses in her essays. It should not startle readers, therefore, to begin this chapter with a discussion of her form, exemplified by her fiction, before investigating her nonfiction.

GAZPACHO: O'CONNOR'S FORM

[William George Clark, Shakespearean scholar] went as a young man to Spain and wrote a pleasant lively account of his holiday called *Gazpacho*: Gazpacho being the name of a certain cold soup which he ate and appears to have enjoyed among the peasants of Andalusia. . . .[1]

When we read O'Connor, we are struck by a similarly pleasant blend, by "objects expertly forged or cast or stamped, with edges, not waxen and worn or softly moulded."[2] The objects are whole, they are real to us. Their form is identifiable. For that reason, we speak of O'Connor's form rather than her style, a term which she undoubtedly assimilated from Cleanth Brooks and Robert Penn Warren's *Understanding Fiction*: "FORM: The arrangement of various elements in a work of literture; the organization of various materials (ideas, images, characters, setting, and the like) to give a single effect."[3]

Her "single effect," the unity of her stories, can be illustrated from "Everything That Rises Must Converge." The story divides conveniently into three stages: before the bus ride, the bus ride, and after the bus ride. In the first part, O'Connor establishes the mother-son relationship and their individual relationships with the past. Even in the first paragraph our picture of Julian's mother takes shape:

She would not ride the buses by herself at night since they had been integrated, and because the reducing class was one of her few pleasures, necessary for her health, and *free*, she said Julian could at least put himself out to take her, considering all she did for him (*CS*, p. 405).

O'Connor provides only those details necessary as catalysts for subsequent action: the exact description of Julian's mother's hat, Julian's hostility toward his mother, her pithy belief that "if you know who you are, you can go anywhere."

After they board the bus, O'Connor uses other passengers—the sandaled woman, a businessman, a woman and her son—as "types" against whose appearances Julian's mother makes her judgments. Her dialogue with some of the passengers contrasts with Julian's interior monologue as he judges her pronouncements and acts contrary to her "druthers." The focal point becomes the hat. A black woman wearing a hat identical to the one Julian's mother has on boards the bus. To overcome her indignation, Julian's mother assumes a condescending attitude toward the black woman's son, Carver. Julian's thoughts anticipate his mother's next act: to offer Carver a nickel.

Upon stepping off the bus, Julian's mother does offer Carver a shiny penny; and Carver's mother strikes Julian's mother in her own fit of indignation. We are well prepared for that act of violence through Julian's mother's comments and through Julian's thoughts. The shock of the blow dazes Julian's mother; but before Julian realizes its effects, he begins lecturing his mother on society's changing nature. Julian then sees that "Her face was fiercely distorted. One eye, large and staring, moved slightly to the left as if it had become unmoored. The other remained fixed on him, raked his face again, found nothing and closed" (*CS*, p. 420). He suddenly is aware of his own situation with all his own prejudices, faults, guilt, and sorrow. At the end we sense through O'Connor's form her concern "with our need of speaking to one another the ultimate confidences, in the exchange of which, only, do we know, and can be, all we as human are—by the ultimate meaning of the word 'human.'"[4]

This story, as are most of O'Connor's stories, is singular because of its form, its merits which Robert Fitzgerald catalogues thus:

. . . no unliving words, the realization of character by exquisitely chosen speech and interior speech and behavior, the action moving at the right speed so that no part of the situation is left out or blurred and the violent thing, though surprising, happens after due preparation, because it has to.[5]

In Wayne C. Booth's words, O'Connor achieves that which gives her readers "a sense, from word to word and line to line, that [she] sees more deeply and judges more profoundly than [her] presented characters."[6] Although we may find her repetition of form predictable, we cannot deny its success, even in varying degrees throughout her twenty-five stories. Nor can we fault her intention to explore with us those awesome mysteries of life.

THE ESSAYS

Her essays, collected and edited by Sally and Robert Fitzgerald in *Mystery and Manners*, provide the most reliable guide to her fiction—to its form and all that we understand that term to imply. Not only do we find them informative, but also we discover that O'Connor is equally entertaining in them as she expresses her beliefs ("sincere convictions") in that same clear style.

Since mere synopsis of the essays seems inevitably doomed to fail because the essays are themselves so readable and so to the point, this discussion will draw readers' attention to their applicability in her fiction. As a companion's aid, it will be more in the form of notes, cross-references, to be referred to while reading the stories.

1. "THE KING OF THE BIRDS"

This essay provides autobiographical background and insight to O'Connor's lifelong interest in peafowl, which, in turn, she uses as symbols as in "The Displaced Person." The peacock in that story becomes a religious symbol, according to Dorothy Walters, as the "emblem of Christ."[7] The priest is the one fascinated with Mrs. McIntyre's peacocks, which are introduced in the second paragraph; and much later in the story, the priest exclaims about the beauty of a peacock with its tail fanned, "Christ will come like that!" (*CS*, p. 226), and then murmurs, "The Transfiguration." From the essay the descriptions of a peacock's physical appearance, habits, and sounds inspire us as closely as they can without our confronting a live peacock. O'Connor infuses her peafowl with personality, a fact which also enhances our understanding of their meaning to her. In short, this essay is to O'Connor's fiction what *Death in the Afternoon* has become to Hemingway's work.

2. "THE FICTION WRITER AND HIS COUNTRY"

O'Connor explains that she picks the word "country" because it is homely and it suggests more—from actual countryside and region to what is "eternal and absolute" (*MM*, p. 27). For O'Connor the eternal and absolute, the meaning of life, is centered in "our Redemption by Christ" (*MM*, p. 32). Thus, she does not see a way for writers to separate mystery from manners, judgment from vision. Moreover, Christian writers will have "the sharpest eyes for the grotesque, for the perverse, and for the unacceptable" (*MM*, p. 33). Why? To demonstrate cause for Redemption in our daily lives. We dealt with this question in the introduction under "subject matter." Mrs. Turpin's hypothetical dilemma about Jesus's giving her a choice between black or white-trash and Mrs. May's constant bickering with Mr. Greenleaf are but two examples.

3. "SOME ASPECTS OF THE GROTESQUE IN SOUTHERN FICTION"

O'Connor identifies three items, any one of which could constitute "grotesqueness" in fiction: an uncommon experience, the use of "mystery," or characters with an invisible burden. We might list immediately examples for each, respectively: "A Good Man Is Hard To Find"; "A View of the Woods," in which Mr. Fortune after looking out at the woods and staring "as if for a prolonged instant he were caught up out of the rattle of everything that led to the future and were held there in the midst of an uncomfortable mystery that he had not apprehended before" (*CS*, p. 348); and Tarwater in *The Violent Bear It Away*. If such characters as Tarwater do come about from novelists' prophetic vision, what do such novelists consider as prophecy? O'Connor defines prophecy as "a matter of seeing near things with their extensions of meaning and thus of seeing far things close up" (*MM*, p. 44). Her definition recalls the image of a telescope, which she uses as symbol in "The Lame Shall Enter First." Prophecy, then, involves seeing, seeing not just the part but the whole; and if novelists have a conception of the whole, they will be able to recognize the grotesque, which is part of the whole.

4. "THE REGIONAL WRITER"

Readers often ask, "What makes a writer 'regional'?" That identity, O'Connor tells us, comes from within a writer, from the knowledge he finds in his community (*MM*, p. 59). All of O'Connor's stories deal with the South. Of the two which rely on setting or experience outside the South—"The Geranium"[8] and "The Enduring Chill"—both draw on the characters' having roots in the South. Most of her stories are Georgia-based. Why the South? Clearly she wrote about the community she knows best, but she offers a subtler explanation:

[Southerners] have gone into the modern world with an inburnt knowledge of human limitations and with a sense of mystery which could not have developed in our first state of innocence [before the Civil War]—as it has not sufficiently developed in the rest of our country (*MM*, p. 59).

". . . the moment when most people are silent." ("The King of the Birds") Photograph by Barbara McKenzie, reprinted by permission of Barbara McKenzie and The Georgia Review.

Taken collectively her stories provide the best description of a regional writer.

5. "THE NATURE AND AIM OF FICTION"

This essay expresses some key ideas about writing that are a basis for O'Connor's form. Art's underpinning is truth, and truth for O'Connor begins with God. Good fiction, she notes, is concrete; and concreteness implies the tangible things in life. For her readers, she recognizes that God is not tangible; therefore, she strives to make His presence felt through the senses, where she says human knowledge begins (*MM*, p. 67). The nature and aim of fiction is the presentation of truth through the senses. Who can understand "good fiction"? The kind of mind "that is willing to have its sense of mystery deepened by contact with reality, and its sense of reality deepened by contact with mystery" (*MM*, p. 79), she replies. In "The Enduring Chill," Asbury is suffering from undulant fever, a reality. O'Connor's problem, as she describes it in a letter dated 25 August 1958 "was to have the Holy Ghost descend by degrees throughout the story but unrecognized, but at the end recognized, coming down, implacable, with ice instead of fire" (*HB*, p. 293), a mystery. Asbury, frozen in humility, has been in bed staring at a water stain on the wallpaper during his illness. O'Connor introduces the stain, and Asbury's focus returns to it again and again until it takes on the meaning she describes in her letter. Thus, it becomes symbol as well, a natural symbol created by what Asbury has imagined as his confrontation with self. The details are selected for a reason, specifically to support the artist's vision, to create movement in the story. On one level, revelation of Asbury's disease is anticlimactic; on a deeper level, Asbury's revelation climaxes his life up to that point. He is, no doubt, a different person spiritually as well as physically. His mother's ironic comment, a gesture of encouragement, is that "it'll keep coming back but it won't kill you!" (*CS*, p. 381). But Asbury has already had the foreboding "that the fate awaiting him was going to be more shattering than any he could have reckoned on" (*CS*, p. 381). That truth is often the aim of O'Connor's fiction.

6. "WRITING SHORT STORIES"

O'Connor defines a "story as a complete dramatic action" (*MM*, p. 90) and identifies the two qualities which make fiction: a sense of mystery and a sense of manners (*MM*, p. 103). She makes these two statements elsewhere as well; and her readers will recognize her practice of them. Her stories, with the exception perhaps of "Why Do the Heathen Rage?," which was to have been part of a third novel, are completed action and end either in death—the end of all life—or abrupt change in the life of a character; mystery prevails either explicitly as Mr. Head and Mr. Fortune realize, or implicitly through unspoken revelation as the child in "A Temple of the

Holy Ghost" demonstrates. And the manners of southern society are everywhere to be found.

7. "ON HER OWN WORK"

O'Connor here identifies her "subject in fiction as the action of grace in territory held largely by the devil" (*MM*, p. 118). This essay deals by example with "A Good Man Is Hard To Find" and *Wise Blood* and offers readers testimony of her direct concern and involvement with the central Christian mysteries. O'Connor also defends her use of violence as an action which returns characters to reality and prepares them to accept their moment of grace.

8. "THE TEACHING OF LITERATURE"

In this essay O'Connor deals with the novel, a genre in which she had produced less and which, in my opinion, she had not established herself. She extends her base—common experience is experience of human limitation (*MM*, p. 131)—to novels and lays down some edicts after taking to task teachers who find ways to avoid teaching literature as literature, e.g., through history, psychology, sociology, and other disciplines. Some of the harm she feels teachers of literature and educators in general have done finds expression in stories such as " The Barber," "A Stroke of Good Fortune," "A Late Encounter with the Enemy," "Good Country People," "The Enduring Chill," "The Comforts of Home," and "The Partridge Festival"—i.e., those stories which reveal "educated" characters without knowledge.

9. "TOTAL EFFECT AND THE EIGHTH GRADE"

O'Connor continues her criticism of modern educational systems that ask students what they will tolerate learning, and she again directs her comments toward literature, specifically toward the ideas that novels should be taught as a subject with a history, that students' taste should be formed, not consulted (*MM*, p. 140).

10. "THE CHURCH AND THE FICTION WRITER"

For O'Connor "the fiction writer presents mystery through manners, grace through nature . . ." (*MM*, p. 153). The Church ensures freedom for the novelist to do so, based on his vision of "What-is."[9] Later she adds, "The Catholic sacramental view of life is one that sustains and supports at every turn the vision that the storyteller must have if he is going to write fiction of any depth" (*MM*, p. 152). It is the sacramental view with which she is concerned.

11. "NOVELIST AND BELIEVER"

Lamenting the loss of faith and belief among modern society, O'Connor sharply parallels the relationship between novelist and believer: whether the novelist believes affects his entire vision, and the way he perceives the world affects what he writes. For example, only when he sees the natural world as good "does evil become intelligible as a destructive force and a necessary result of our freedom" (*MM*, p. 157). Separation of the two, of the material and the abstract, approaches Manichaeanism, which expresses belief that salvation lies in the release of goodness and a return to the original state of separation of spirit and matter.[10] O'Connor, of course, does not separate the two, and she combines the sacramental view and the nature effectively in such stories as "The River" and *The Violent Bear It Away*. If grace is cut off from nature or if its possibility is denied, artists cannot have it operating in their stories. The burden then rests with both writer and reader, and the answer for "great religious fiction" is the combination of believing artist and believing society.

12. "CATHOLIC NOVELISTS AND THEIR READERS"

O'Connor defines a "Catholic novel" as "one that represents reality adequately as we see it manifested in this world of things and human relationships. Only in and by these sense experiences does the fiction writer approach a contemplative knowledge of the mystery they embody" (*MM*, p. 172). The novelist assumes the responsibility of creating an illusion of a complete world with believable people; that world for the Catholic novelist is founded on theological truths—the Fall, the Redemption, and the Judgment. The reader, too, must assume some responsibility; he must be willing to accept the novelist as artist, must accept his limitations, and must be brave enough to confront truth. As she has already pointed out in earlier essays, the two are not equally and mutually prepared for one another. The Catholic reader usually makes one big mistake: he believes that the Catholic novelist is writing for him (*MM*, p. 185). The novelist writes for himself and tries to make what he writes art by adhering to strict standards, not of religion but of art. If his art is true, O'Connor asserts, his "message" is apt to be true too.

This essay is perhaps in response to the continual misreadings her works suffered, and in fact continue to suffer. Her concerns over misconceptions about Catholicism and over a lack of faith overall are exemplified in her stories, essays, and letters. Her understanding of the relationship between art and religion is singular in modern letters, as this essay properly attests.

13. "THE CATHOLIC NOVELIST IN THE PROTESTANT SOUTH"

Rather than being mutually exclusive, both Catholic and Southern literature share a sense of tradition and reinforce one another. The Catholic has the "ability to resist the dissolution of belief," and can bolster the South's best traditions; and the South has more respect for the concrete, more trust in blind imagination, and can make the Catholic less timid as a novelist (*MM*, p. 208). The milieu of the South and the faith of the Catholic, O'Connor believes, will be a happy combination for both in the future. O'Connor herself has blended the best of both, although the truths she reveals are not always to her readers' liking.

14. "INTRODUCTION TO *A MEMOIR OF MARY ANN*"

Because the entire essay is reprinted in Appendix 2 and is therefore readily available to users of this book, I shall keep my remarks brief. Two comments, however, should be made. One is the fact that O'Connor refers directly and often to Hawthorne, especially to his story "The Birthmark." Hawthorne's stories face some of the difficult problems with which O'Connor's stories deal—moral versus immoral, good versus evil, salvation versus damnation. Critics have already written on some of these similarities, but they do not seem to have exhausted this comparison yet. The other comment concerns O'Connor's explanation of the Communion of Saints, "created upon human imperfection, created from what we make of our grotesque state" (*MM*, p. 228). We have referred to "grotesqueness" enough by now that that subject should require no further amplification. This essay addresses the subject from a slightly different angle—real life; and it brings into focus earlier remarks by O'Connor about the purpose of fiction and its necessity to draw on human limitations. Readers who have held O'Connor's feelings toward children suspect can, based on this essay alone, allay their fears. Sensitive readers will recognize the compassion and admiration that O'Connor holds for Mary Ann.

POSTSCRIPT

The Fitzgeralds explain that the essays selected for inclusion in *Mystery and Manners* were drawn largely from lectures which O'Connor gave and subsequently published between 1957 and 1963. Her essays are second only to her short fiction in form, grace, and clarity. O'Connor has that knack for stating what she wants to say and then for saying it in a way that entertains at the same time that it informs. The anecdotes, such as the lineman who encounters the peacock (*MM*, p. 11), are earmarks of a gifted storyteller and writer.

Flannery O'Connor is unusual among her peers because her essays speak with the same honesty and forthrightness of her fiction. She knew what she was about and where she was going and was not afraid to share that information with interested inquirers. She did not worry about giving away trade secrets as many writers do. She wanted her audience to be informed, to achieve that level of understanding necessary for "great religious fiction." The mystery for her is not in the fiction but in the subject of fiction: in life and in man's relation to God. The process of fiction she explained as well as anyone has, and she was not embarrassed to do so. Consequently, her essays have become an integral part of her very small canon.

3

The Fiction

That Flannery O'Connor seems to have written her stories according to a recipe may be the result of her master's degree program at the University of Iowa, that is, of a formal training that could not help but channel imaginative energy. Practically speaking, writing programs must create an atmosphere in which their students can produce manuscripts, and productivity necessitates regimentation. Writing requires discipline; good writing demands it. O'Connor's finely tailored stories reflect her habit of discipline just as her letters record that fact.

O'Connor's first paragraphs are masterpieces in miniature. They introduce major characters, central conflicts, and controlling images; and they establish the relationships necessary for the development of the stories. Most importantly they capture readers' interest by raising key questions. Why is it difficult for liberals in Dilton ("The Barber")? Why would azalea blossoms have a lethal effect on Calhoun ("The Partridge Festival")? Where is Hazel Motes going (*Wise Blood*)?

O'Connor's characters are compilations of purposeful details which reveal the characters' personality traits. Their very actions provide us with mental pictures of them invariably more vivid than direct statement. To say that a child is spoiled, for example, is to offer a flat, uninteresting fact; but to have a child act spoiled is to create for readers a "living" person. Who can forget John Wesley and June Star, the children in "A Good Man Is Hard To Find"? The physical descriptions of O'Connor's characters match their personalities or, like caricatures in cartoons, exaggerate incongruities: the "feline empty eyes" of the nymphomaniac in "The Comforts of Home," or Mrs. Shortley's mountainous frame in "The Displaced Person."

After reading a few O'Connor stories, we anticipate those patterns and learn to attend more closely to the clues she provides. We start listening to what the characters say and weighing what they say against how they act—not only how they act toward other people, but also how they react to their environment. We notice, too, that more times than not certain words carry double meanings. The adjective "good" often sets us up for a reversal or for an ironic truth: a good man is indeed hard to find.

An O'Connor story builds on recurring images (details) which have their essential place in the literal level of the story and which operate in depth as well as on the surface, increasing the story in every direction (*MM*, p. 71). As they accrue, they become symbols which allow the meaning of the story to keep expanding for readers, the more they think about it.[1] In "The Enduring Chill" the water stain which Asbury stares at takes on the image of a fierce bird which becomes a symbol of the Holy Ghost (*CS*, p. 382). Technological imagery (trains, automobiles, bulldozers, telescopes) seems to promise "to expand the capacity of the human person for life and happiness";[2] animal imagery (birds, pigs, parrots, cats) offers insights into characters' inner being or becomes tangible manifestations of the supernatural;[3] and clothing imagery (hats, shoes, eye glasses) and color imagery (lavender in particular) may signal the wearer's intentions and therefore become symbols of the presence of good or evil.[4]

I recognize the danger in lumping together images in general categories and hasten to remind readers of what O'Connor has said about symbols. The images become symbols only if within the context of the story they accrue special meanings that operate validly at a deeper level for the reader. All of this construct functions as Howard C. Brashers has described the creative process: "Language brings us to style [or form], style to choice, choice to the variety and complexity of technique, technique finally to meaning and theme."[5] But meaning, O'Connor says, "cannot be captured in an interpretation" (*HB*, p. 437). How then do we understand a story's meaning? By consideration of the whole.

Forewarned and forearmed, we shall explore O'Connor's twenty-five short stories[6] and two novels. At the end of each discussion is a list of other stories that seem to me to be closely related to the one at hand; and the selected bibliography refers to other, more detailed discussions of most of the stories.

THE SHORT STORIES

The first "three" stories—"The Geranium," "An Exile in the East," and "Judgement Day"—are really three versions of the same story. They represent roughly the beginning, middle, and end of O'Connor's writing career, appearing in 1946, 1954, and 1964, respectively.[7] The first and third frame her collection of stories, published posthumously; the second was first published in the *South Carolina Review* in 1978. In the following discussions they are considered separately but counted as one story.

1a. "THE GERANIUM"

This story is about relationships: human relationships on the broadest scale, familial relationships on a narrower scale, and spiritual relationships on an individual scale. Simply paraphrased, the story involves a father from Georgia who has gone to live with his daughter and son-in-law in New York City. They live in a tenement building in overcrowded, impoverished conditions which help create tension and unhappiness for Old Dudley. He wants to return to Georgia, but cannot and is reminded of "home" by a sickly geranium which the "neighbors" across the alley sun regularly each day. Of course there is more to it than that.

In her first paragraph O'Connor establishes the context of the story: like the geranium that "shouldn't have been there," Old Dudley is out of place in the sterile environment of the city. His life there is one of passiveness without meaning; his one "activity" is watching those people fifteen feet away, six floors up in the adjacent building. The pattern of the story is repetitive and predictable: like Proustian tea and madeleines,[8] the geranium sends Old Dudley's thoughts back to Georgia after each unpleasant incident he encounters. We witness the incidents, his thoughts about the geranium (no flower at all), and his remembrances of things past. In each set more is revealed about his varied relationships.

The relationship between Old Dudley and his daughter is at best strained. The bases of that strain are Old Dudley's overwhelming pride (hubris) and the daughter's change in values, both of which are revealed through setting. Through the omniscient narrator, we learn that living in New York City is "tight." Not only is it tight, it is complicated for a man like Old Dudley. Instead of being provider, protector, and a source of knowledge as he was in Georgia at the boarding house, Old Dudley is dependent on his daughter, is afraid of the building itself—the "dog runs" and the men in undershirts who might growl at him—and is ignorant of the ways of the city. He is not in control, nor is he in command.

His daughter, on the other hand, has forsaken the ways in which she was "raised": she lives "tight with niggers," does her "duty" toward her father grudgingly, married a city boy who drives trucks and shows signs of rootlessness, and even speaks harshly to her father. Her world, her apartment, is "too tight," the hallway runs like a tape measure with the doors as inch marks. What had seemed like an important place to Old Dudley's romanticized notion, based on the movie *Big Town Rhythm*, is actually nowhere with no room, too tight. This life-style and the people in it his daughter accepts. Her advice to Old Dudley that he should "tend to his own business" echoes his thoughts in the opening paragraph that "they had no business with it [the geranium], no business with it" and foreshadows the geranium owner's words that what he does in his apartment is his own business.

In Georgia Old Dudley's own business was the business of everyone else: the old ladies' "sparrow-like wars," Rabie's whereabouts and goings on, the Grisby boy's daily routine—all were part of the community which Old Dudley was very much a part of. His relationship with the old ladies of the boarding house was one of provider (the fish he caught each Wednesday), and protector ("he was the man in the house"), a role they accepted and even expected him to play. Contrarily, he is met by indifference from women tenants in the apartment building: Mrs. Schmitt sends the pattern to the door by one of her children who does not speak; and the fat woman on the stairs, the one who reminds him of Mrs. Benson back home, does not even speak as she squeezes past him.

Old Dudley's relationship with blacks is also reversed in New York City. For Rabie back in Georgia, he was "master," a source of knowledge about mechanical things (guns), and a ruler of Rabie's life. Rabie allows that. The "nigger with the shiny tan shoes" in the apartment building is just the opposite: he talks of guns, helps Old Dudley, and ironically is the only other person to offer kind words and support (literally) in Old Dudley's time of need. The roles switch. Old Dudley's pride again manifests itself in the constriction in his throat.[9]

The "neighbor's" good deed is quickly abated by the geranium owner's mockingly hostile exchange with Old Dudley. No kind words, no peace, no quiet for Old Dudley as he inquires about the geranium's whereabouts. His moment of reconciliation past, Old Dudley has alienated the spiritual relationship as well. He cannot speak. He can only stare down six floors at the uprooted geranium and cry.

For Old Dudley the cracked flowerpot and broken geranium symbolize his final loss of touch with his community, although two people tell him how to get along in the city: his daughter tells him to mind his own business, advice generally well meant; and the neighbor tells him that "it's a swell place once you get use to it"—similar advice without explicit instruction.

1b. "AN EXILE IN THE EAST"

According to Jan Nordby Gretlund, who introduces the first publication of this story, "An Exile in the East" avoids "the sentimentality of 'The Geranium' and virtually all the melodrama of 'Judgement Day' . . . the heavy symbolism of the first story and . . . the manifest theology of [the]

*"She lived in a building—the middle in a row of
buildings all alike, all blackened-red and gray with
rasp-mouthed people hanging out their windows. . . ."
("The Geranium")
George Wesley Bellows, American
1882-1925, Cliff Dwellers, 1913 oil on canvas
(39½" x 41½"), reproduced with permission of
Los Angeles County Museum of Art (#16.4):
Los Angeles County funds.*

last story. Above all [it] treats the racial theme in greater depth than the other [two] stories."[10] His comparison among the three stories highlights important scenes to illustrate that "Flannery O'Connor could be sociological as well as theological."[11]

Old Dudley becomes Old Tanner and Rabie becomes Coleman in the last two stories; and the changes between the first and second stories are more pronounced than the changes between the second and third. By 1963-64 O'Connor has added a black landlord, Dr. Foley, whose pressure on Tanner to run his still helps Tanner decide to go to New York with his daughter. Although the daughter's character is slightly more developed in the last two stories, it is basically as we discern it in "The Geranium": grudgingly obligatory toward Tanner.

The major addition to this story is the flashback to Tanner's meeting Coleman. The scene is a showdown of sorts. Coleman, new around the sawmill, challenges Tanner by not working and hence stirring up resentment among the other workers. The climactic focus becomes a ridiculous pair of "spectacles" Tanner whittles from pine bark. Through "improved vision" Coleman is better able to see his position and their relationship in the community. From this episode we can appreciate two aspects of Tanner's personality: his feelings toward blacks are abundantly clear, and his authority in Georgia versus his dependency in New York represents a tremendous fall for him. O'Connor leaves this sawmill scene in "Judgement Day" also.

1c. "JUDGEMENT DAY"

Not only do the names change, but also the relationships change in that they are heightened and accented by more characterization, although setting still plays a significant role in supporting theme. Tanner's daughter is revealed as a proud, selfish woman who much like the daughter in "The Geranium" is doing her "duty" grudgingly and maybe for her father's pension checks. We also get a better glimpse of the son-in-law's character, still rootless, but more mocking and critical of his father-in-law's plight. He is the one who "just wants to make sure" the daughter plans to ignore her promise to bury Tanner back in Corinth, Georgia.

The daughter is also more in control in "Judgement Day." Physically, her father is less able to care for himself, and therefore even the menial task of dressing him falls to her. She even dictates when he goes to the bathroom, and she receives and spends his pension check: "it'll just pay the first two weeks' doctor-bill," she tells him. He is in fact her "prisoner," a position underscored by O'Connor in the final scene when Tanner is found dead on the stairs with his feet dangling over the stairwell like "those of a man in the stocks."

Tanner's relationship with blacks is governed by the philosophy that "the secret of handling a nigger was to show him his brains didn't have a chance against yours." His domination of Coleman Parrum for thirty years was based on just that. But Foley, part black, the rest Indian and white, becomes for Tanner an intermediate position: he could be a "nigger's white nigger" for Foley rather than a nothing in no-place, i.e., in New York City. The third position in his relationship with blacks is one of complete dependence. The black actor, his daughter's neighbor, does not fall for his "preacher" greetings; and indeed Tanner's "brains" simply do not have a chance against the actor's. Thus, the actor completely dominates Tanner who ironically does not understand him at all, and he reacts violently to Tanner's condescending attitude. At first, he merely shoves Tanner back into the daughter's apartment, hurt but still alive. The second encounter, after Tanner's fall (both literally and figuratively), again humiliates Tanner and results in his demise. But Tanner, just before his death, asks the black for help: "Hep me up, Preacher. I'm on my way home!" A semiredemptive gesture on Tanner's part?[12]

Earlier, before the daughter goes out, Tanner momentarily feels guilty, a sign of admission to himself that he "had been nothing but a nuisance to her" and that she has been good to him. That we are told by the narrator. The moment is quickly undercut by his reaction to the "lie" he tells his daughter as he tries to "kill the outrageous taste" his lie creates in his mouth. So again, the old father rejects his moment of grace, his chance for reconciliation. He does not change in his own self-relationship. Nor should he as far as the story goes. He is, in that way, consistent throughout.

According to Ralph C. Wood, however:

the entire action of the story bears this affirmation out [that Tanner has made his way home]: Tanner has confessed his sin (albeit unwittingly in a series of remembrances meant to justify his racial pride), received his judgment, done his penance, and thus gone to his eternal destiny well prepared.[13]

Hardly. Tanner does make his way home only after the daughter suffers pangs of guilt because she has broken her promise to her father, an act which suggests she does have a conscience and a tie back home after all. Tanner's "confessions" are undercut by his egregious pride and lack of conviction; his "judgment" is precisely his moment of racial pride when he catches up to his daughter, thereby escaping Foley, an act for which he later repents; and his "penance," his admission that his daughter is good, is also undercut by his comment about his being a liar. Instead of being well-prepared, he meets death at the hands of fate, as a result of his trying to negotiate the stairs when he is physically unprepared to do so. Mentally, he is prepared to die trying, an attitude which reflects his pride. His appearance of being in stocks can be interpreted as his own self-imprisonment to that pride. His reliance on the actor at the very end becomes as futile as the grandmother's "moment" with the Misfit.

OTHER CITY-COUNTRY STORIES: "A Stroke of Good Fortune," The Artificial Nigger," and "Everything That Rises Must Converge."

2. "THE BARBER"

Rayber, a college teacher, is the butt of this story. Joe, the barber, passes small talk with Rayber during the first of three visits which Rayber makes to the barbershop: weather, hunting, and finally politics. It is an election year. Darmon, a liberal, versus Hawkson, a southern Democrat. Joe, his friend Roy, and most of the other townspeople are for "Hawk" who is against "niggers." Joe baits Rayber who takes the discussion seriously. The first visit, Rayber does not say the right words; the second, he has rehearsed how the previous conversation should have gone but is stumped when asked for some reasons why anyone should vote for Darmon; and the third visit, he returns fully prepared for an elaborate "speech" full of sound and fury, but signifying nothing. Through the chortling of the other patrons, especially Roy, Rayber is provoked to violence. He hits Joe and storms out not to return, a fact we are told in the second sentence of the story.

Although the discussion of politics centers on the question of race, the thematic thrust of the story centers on Rayber's place in the community as an "intellectual." He is accepted. Joe says, "He's all right, doesn't know how to vote, but he's all right." Joe's statement, the grinning nature of the "discussion," and George's (the shine boy's) reaction to the entire episode are lost on Rayber who, unlike his colleague Jacobs, cannot come to grips with his own mind and position. The effect on Joe and the others is zero; on Rayber, complete humiliation. A different moment of "grace," one of social amenity, is lost on Rayber, the white knight on the black charger. Rayber suffers what Eric Voegelin calls "disorder of the soul," that is, a "failure to grasp the new truth of order and to become attuned to it."[14]

The story is not overly subtle and contains, via Joe, some of the stereotypes of blacks in the South. Rayber has had trouble with his position in the community, not just the small southern town but also the larger community of intellectual ideas.

OTHER STORIES ABOUT "INTELLECTUALS": "Good Country People," "The Enduring Chill," "The Comforts of Home," "Everything That Rises Must Converge," "The Partridge Festival," "Why Do the Heathen Rage?" and The Violent Bear It Away.

3. "WILDCAT"

"Wildcat" is unique among O'Connor's writing because it is the only story from the black point of view, solely about blacks, and mostly in dialogue. It is reminiscent of William Faulkner's little story "That Evening Sun," in which Nancy sits waiting for Jesus, her estranged husband, to return and kill her. Like O'Connor's Gabriel, Nancy is reconciled to dying.[15] What they both want is death on their own terms.

Old Gabriel, a blind black, has the sense of smell for a rampaging wildcat (symbol of the angel of death) that he knows is coming for him—if not tonight, then the next. The contrast is between the boys (youth) who go out after the cat and Old Gabriel (age) who is willing to wait for it to come to him. His vision of the Lord waiting for him with golden vestments suggests to the reader that the wildcat (death) will get him just as it got Hezuh when Gabe was a boy. His wish is to die as a man, instead of waiting with women for death to steal him away.

4. "THE CROP"

Another early story in which O'Connor experiments with subject matter and form, "The Crop" may be read with two different purposes in mind: to learn about the fictional character, Miss Willerton, and to infer what O'Connor is saying about writers in general.

In the humdrum life of Miss Willerton, age forty-four, the only "excitement" she enjoys is escaping via her rather limited imagination (her search for topics about which to write suggests how limited). When she meets her fantasy face-to-face on the street (the couple she passes fits her description of her fictional sharecroppers), she does not recognize it. She is more interested in escaping life than in dealing with it, a tendency contrary to a "good" writer's interest according to O'Connor. Miss Willerton's absorption with her fantasy is marked by her entering the story and in her imagination becoming Lot's wife.[16] Familial relationships play a tangential role in that family members intrude on Willie's[17] world with mundane demands: crumbing the table and going to the grocery store.

Finally, it is O'Connor's use (her only use) of the story-within-a-story technique that interests us in studying her canon. Notwithstanding the fact that the irony is heavy-handed and that the characters are not well-drawn, it is an amusingly conceived story and reveals that in 1946 O'Connor's artistic ability was beginning a transition from cartooning to storytelling.

OTHER STORIES ABOUT WOMEN ALONE: "A Circle in the Fire," "The Displaced Person," "Good Country People," "Greenleaf," "The Comforts of Home," and "Everything That Rises Must Converge."

5. "THE TURKEY"

Originally entitled "The Capture," this story subtly shows an eleven-year-old's initiation into the world of good and evil. Ruller's thoughts dominate the story as he plays a game of cowboys with his imaginary friends (opening paragraph). It is a game of violence with "good guys" and "bad guys" and guns and with good triumphing in the end. But Ruller is distracted by the sight of a wild turkey, which he chases. His motivation is to risk his parents' anger over a torn shirt for pride over his accomplishment: bringing home a turkey for the dinner table. Ironically, when the bird, wounded and therefore not as difficult a prey as Ruller first believes, eludes capture, Ruller denies Grace. He thinks of his brother Hane, a juvenile delinquent, and takes pleasure in swearing and defying his parents and grandmother, although in reality he is angry because he has run into a tree and knocked the wind out of himself. When his thoughts return to his condition, he spies the turkey, dead from loss of blood; Ruller believes that the turkey is a sign from God and repents. Again his pride manifests itself, and he takes the long way home, through town on Saturday afternoon, to allow all to see his capture. Moved by the experience, he asks God to send him a beggar so that he can give the beggar his only dime (sacrifice). Hetty Gilman, the town's beggar, appears mysteriously from nowhere, and Ruller thrusts the dime in her hand and feels an uplifting Grace—a feeling he has never felt before. Then he encounters another evil force—the country boys—who betray him and steal his turkey. Now afraid that "Something Awful was tearing behind him with its arms rigid and its fingers ready to clutch," Ruller runs home. His fear of evil, however, can be taken as a sign that his experience was "unusual" and that he has been initiated into the larger condition of man.

Sister Kathleen Feeley observes about that greater truth: "that God works through reality according to His own designs, not man's."[18] She also notes that this story marks the beginnings of O'Connor's "varied explorations of a child's apprehension of reality."

OTHER STORIES OF INITIATION: "The Life You Save May Be Your Own," "The River," "A Temple of the Holy Ghost," "The Artificial Nigger," "The Lame Shall Enter First," and *The Violent Bear It Away.*

6. "A STROKE OF GOOD FORTUNE"

The "stroke of good fortune" is ironically exactly what Ruby does not want: a baby. The signs are there throughout the story. She has trouble climbing stairs, is always short of breath, has swollen ankles, and has gained weight. Also, her reflections on her brother Rufus, her attitude toward Hartley Gilfeet (the child from the sixth floor), Madam Zoleeda's prediction, Laverne Watt's words, and Bill Hill's smile—all suggest what Ruby is unwilling to admit.

The setting is the staircase of Ruby's apartment building and her ascent which, by the way, she never completes. (The story was first published as "A Woman on the Stairs.")

Ruby is characterized as a proud, even vain woman who thinks of herself at thirty-four as young: her interest in Mr. Jerger's reference to Ponce de

Leon and the fountain of youth flags her concern over staying young, and she admits that she touches up her grey hair. Another aspect of her pride appears in her independence; she prides herself in never having been to a physician. She feels that she "made something of herself" by getting out of Pitman, by marrying a traveling salesman of "Miracle Products," and by not having children in five years of marriage.

She disparages her in-laws, her brother,[19] and her neighbors. She dreams of a house in suburbia, in Meadowcrest Heights—a pipe dream in view of the impending expense of a baby. When she becomes painfully aware of the truth—a feeling "as if it were out nowhere in nothing, out nowhere, resting and waiting, with plenty of time"—Ruby collapses on the stairs in abject misery.

This story marks for me O'Connor's first measurable growth as a writer. Away from institutional restrictions and with the confidence of a published author, she seems to have a firmer grasp on the direction her writing is taking. In retrospect, however, she wrote the Fitzgeralds about this story: "It is, in its way, Catholic, being about the rejection of life at the source, but too much of a farce to bear the weight . . ." (*HB*, p. 85). "A Stroke of Good Fortune" is, at least, an important transition between her early work and her more mature writing.

OTHER STORIES OF MARITAL RELATIONSHIPS: "A Good Man Is Hard to Find," "Revelation," and "Parker's Back."

7. "A GOOD MAN IS HARD TO FIND"

"A Good Man Is Hard to Find" is a compelling piece and one of the most written about in the O'Connor canon. The story itself centers on familial relationships, in particular the son-mother relationship. Bailey's mother, "the grandmother," lives with him, his wife, and their three children in Atlanta, Georgia—a typically suburban family not unlike the ones we find in John Cheever's stories and in Joseph Heller's *Something Happened*. John Wesley and June Star are both spoiled, disrespectful brats who sass their elders and whine for their way. The mother is nondescript; she wears her hair in a rabbit-eared kerchief and has a face "as innocent as a cabbage."

The grandmother dominates characterization and is the motivating force throughout the story. She suggests the detour down the dirt road, she secretly takes the cat Pitty Sing that ultimately causes the accident, and she recognizes the Misfit thereby ensuring their demise. She is in many ways a stereotype: cautious (let's don't go to Florida) when it serves her purpose (she wants to go to Tennessee); devious (takes the cat and fabricates a story to work her way about the detour); and vain (dresses for the trip, calls the Misfit a "good person," and thinks back to her earlier days). The Misfit sums up her character, though, when he says, "She would of been a good woman if it had been somebody there to shoot her every minute of her life."[20]

The other character to whom we direct most of our attention is the Misfit. We learn more about him than any other character: his "crime" which he does not remember but for which the authorities have the papers, his family, and his attitude toward Jesus who, he says, threw everything out of balance. Of course, he is not a "good" man; he is a cold-blooded killer who executes six members of a family including two children and an infant. When he states, "there's just meanness," we believe that he is sincere. We should pay close attention to his statements because they fulfill two other purposes: they are foil to the grandmother's hypocrisy and illuminate her character as a "lady" and they make a statement about latter-day Christians.

Structurally the story takes three turns: departure from Atlanta and the trip to Red Sammy's, the detour and accident, and the encounter with the Misfit.

Symbolically the story is rather heavy-handed at times, for example, the Misfit's arriving in a black hearse, the woods which appear to open wide like a mouth, and Bailey's shirt—all of which gather meaning as the story progresses.

Thematically it brings to light O'Connor's concern with an individual's moment of grace, which she glosses for Andrew Lytle in these terms:

the Grandmother recognizes the Misfit as one of her own children and reaches out to touch him. It's the moment of grace for her anyway—a silly old woman—but it leads him to shoot her. This moment of grace excites the devil to frenzy (*HB*, p. 373).[21]

Because the characterizations are more fully drawn, the relationships better defined and motivated, and the message clearly unified and more succinct, "A Good Man Is Hard to Find" is a benchmark in O'Connor's development as a master of short fiction.

OTHER STORIES ABOUT FAMILIES: "A Late Encounter with the Enemy," "A View of the Woods," "The Enduring Chill," "The Comforts of Home," "Everything That Rises Must Converge," "Why Do the Heathen Rage?," *Wise Blood*, and *The Violent Bear It Away*.

8. "A LATE ENCOUNTER WITH THE ENEMY"

The event is the graduation of Sally Poker Sash, age 62, from college; the "star" is General "Tennessee Flintrock" Sash, age 104, Sally's grandfather. We learn that Sally has endured for twenty years the heat of the Georgia summer[22] to finish her degree—not to become a better teacher, but to show everyone what she comes from. The general's claim to fame, rather than his longevity and the fact that he is one of the few living veterans of the Civil

"Outside of Toombsboro she woke up and recalled an old plantation that she had visited in this neighborhood once. . . ." ("A Good Man Is Hard to Find") Photograph by the author.

War, is his attending the premiere of *Gone with the Wind* in Atlanta some twelve years earlier and his being around the "pretty guls."

Sally ironically muses to herself that she hopes he will live at least until her graduation, which he just does do. John Wesley Poker Sash, Boy Scout age ten, wheels his great-grandfather in for the ceremony at which the old general envisions "a black hole" opening in his head. Sally's character is vain and overflowing with self-esteem and accomplishment; John Wesley is typical of what has become O'Connor's stereotype of children—disrespectful, self-centered, and sometimes downright hateful.

The grandfather represents age and a link with the past, although O'Connor mentions several times the insignificance of history to him. He *is* history. How is he treated? As artifact for special occasions at which time he is placed on display, not unlike the "shrunken man" in *Wise Blood*. Thus, O'Connor seems to be making a point about modern man's treatment of history and his past, echoed perhaps in the graduation speaker's statement: "If we forget our past, we won't remember our future and it will be as well for we won't have one." Past and future may be the same thing to General Sash, but should not be to the graduates. As the graduates are hearing that speech, the general is encountering "the enemy"—the figure in the black robe firing words "at him like musket" balls. He clenches his sword until the blade touches bone, and he dies on stage as the graduates file past to receive their diplomas. The general again upstages his granddaughter's accomplishment, but her vision of what has transpired is blurred by her egocentricity.

OTHER STORIES ABOUT THE PAST: "The Geranium," "The Comforts of Home," "Everything That Rises Must Converge," "The Partridge Festival," and *Wise Blood*.

9. "THE LIFE YOU SAVE MAY BE YOUR OWN"

Though simple on the surface, this story is perplexing in several ways: the mother's relationship with her daughter Lucynell; Shiftlet's attitude about the human condition (he is after all a heartless con man); the last scene with the guffawing thunder. Basically, shiftless Shiftlet wanders onto the Crater place, talks his way into work, marries the daughter for convenience (to get Mrs. Crater's money and a car, which he has always wanted), abandons the idiot-daughter, and flees to Mobile.

Shiftlet's question "What is a man?" has faint echoes from *Hamlet* (II.ii.303), and his talk about the human heart (referred to twice) brings to mind Hawthorne's "Young Goodman Brown." The symbolism of money and material gain versus spiritual well being (man is made of body and spirit Shiftlet tells Mrs. Crater), the references to Lucynell as an angel and an innocent, and the metaphor of Shiftlet's smile like a snake combine to suggest the Garden-Temptation motif. (That Shiftlet refers to his mother as an angel of God does not weaken the argument for him as devil if one accepts the idea that the devil is a fallen angel.) But when wily evil (Shiftlet) meets with cynical youth (hitchhiker), he does not fool him and is told ironically to go to the devil by the youth who wants no part of the devil.

Another hint of devilry also comes from Shiftlet. When he is about to sleep in Mrs. Crater's car, Shiftlet makes a reference to the monks who slept in their coffins. Coupled with the moon imagery, we are reminded mentally that vampires slept in their coffins, too. Shiftlet very patiently sucks the lifeblood (Lucynell) from Mrs. Crater.[23]

Mr. Shiftlet's dissatisfaction arises when Mrs. Crater refers to him as a disabled tramp, at the marriage ceremony (one of the sacraments), after he drops Lucynell at The Hot Spot, and after the hitchhiker jumps out of the car. That is, after Shiftlet suffers loss. Loss for evil is gain for good. Delivering Lucynell to the roadside cafe, The Hot Spot (hell), does not give Shiftlet (the devil) satisfaction. Hers is just one more soul out of how many? For each gain, there seems to be a loss (hitchhiker). As O'Connor notes, "there is nothing more relating to the mystery of that man's personality that could be shown through that particular dramatization" (*MM*, p. 94).

Who are the "slime" Shiftlet asks to be washed from this earth? On one level, they are the ones who insult Shiftlet, Mrs. Crater and the hitchhiker. On another level, though, slime like beauty must be in the eye of the beholder. For Shiftlet, they are the pure, the innocent, those who are not led into temptation.

OTHER STORIES ABOUT DEVILRY: "A Good Man Is Hard to Find," "The River," "Good Country People," "A View of the Woods," "The Comforts of Home," "The Lame Shall Enter First," "Revelation," and *The Violent Bear It Away*.

10. "THE RIVER"

Another (the second) from a child's point of view about the world in which he lives is "The River." Harry Ashfield, a "little" boy, has parents who do not seem to care for him. They give parties, enjoy getting him out of the way, and spend very little time with him. Mrs. Connin, Harry's sitter for a day, does care. She takes Harry to her house where she feeds him, to the river where a preacher named Bevel baptizes him, and back to his apartment where he faces the aftermath of his parents' party.

At Mrs. Connin's house Harry lets loose one of her shoats because her children trick him. What Harry learns, however, is that pigs are not as he has been told from storybooks—pink, fat, curly-tailed, and wearing bow ties; rather they are gray, dirty, and smelly. He becomes acquainted with a reality of life.

At the river he is baptized and hears Bevel's words about a river of life and the Kingdom of Christ, words he does not comprehend. Contrasted with the scene at the river is the return to his parents' apartment: bottles, full ashtrays, clutter. Harry awakens before his parents, who suffer from hangovers, and returns alone to the river where he will "count." His attitude is not unlike Ruller's ("The Turkey") at first because when the river does not accept him, he gets angry and thrashes about. Harry is then caught by the current and swept away. Mr. Paradise, a nonbeliever who had heckled Bevel the day before, is unable to save him although he tries: he emerges from the river "like some ancient water monster . . . empty-handed."

That is the structural outline of "The River." It is a story of contrasts: Mrs. Connin and the Ashfields, Harry and Mrs. Connin's children, Bevel and Mr. Paradise, light and dark, city and country. It uses some of O'Connor's stock-in-trade imagery: water, pigs, automobile, and colors. The alienation that Harry feels at home motivates him to seek the river of life. Even Mr. Paradise's bribe of candy does not deter him; his life has changed just as Bevel promised. His sins of lying and stealing are expiated through baptism; but only after he feels the river taking him under does he relax and believe that he is "getting somewhere."

OTHER STORY ABOUT BAPTISM: *The Violent Bear It Away.*

11. "A CIRCLE IN THE FIRE"

Mrs. Cope, widow and owner of the farm, is visited by one of her former employee's sons, Powell Boyd, and two of Powell's friends from Atlanta. She is rigidly polite to the boys and does not want them to stay. They stay and cause mischief which results in their setting fire to Mrs. Cope's woods. Vandalism, however, is ostensibly the subject of "A Circle in the Fire."

In O'Connor's canon, Mrs. Cope begins a long line of single-women characters who have to shoulder the burden of rearing a child, running a farm, and "coping" with life in general. Mrs. Cope does not cope well with her hired hands, the Pritchards; the uninvited visitors; her Negroes; her fat little twelve-year-old daughter, Sally Virginia; and the weeds and nut grass. Her fear is fire, referenced early in the story and with supporting imagery building toward the inevitable conclusion. Mrs. Pritchard is another stereotype in O'Connor's fiction: the opposite of Mrs. Cope, not pretty, more down to earth, lazy, superstitious—a foil to Mrs. Cope's ways. She functions as the little voice of doom with which Mrs. Cope must contend as she repeatedly reminds everyone how much they have to be thankful for.

The last sentence in this story helps blend imagery and theme into a satisfactory whole:

[Sally Virginia] stood taut, listening, and could just catch in the distance a few wild high shrieks of joy as if the prophets were dancing in the fiery furnace, in the circle the angel [Mrs. Cope?] had cleared for them.

A circle carries symbolic meaning in both Christianity and witchcraft; the scene O'Connor describes is clearly demonic, though. We ask, why Mrs. Cope? Is she being chastised because of her pride? Or like Job, is she simply being tested for no apparent reason at all? We might argue convincingly either way, and still we must face the fact that Mrs. Cope does not handle forces of destruction well—"her Negroes," nut grass, the boys—when confronted directly by them.

There is something else going on beneath the surface story of Mrs. Cope's suffering. Sally Virginia is at that awkward age between child's fantasy (dressing up to play "cowboys") and adolescent's reality in all its starkness. The second part of the story is devoted to Sally Virginia's playing in the woods. There she spies on the three boys, naked and hateful. After they set fire to the brush, she tries to run across the field; but "her legs were too heavy and she stood there, weighted down with some new unplaced misery that she had never felt before": recognition of evil and her first menstruation. A flood of new "truths" covers Sally Virginia as she joins her mother and looks at her "face of the new misery she felt." One of Mrs. Cope's burdens may, at that point, be lifted.

OTHER STORIES ABOUT MOTHER-DAUGHTER RELATIONSHIPS: "The Life You Save May Be Your Own," "A Temple of the Holy Ghost," and "Good Country People."

12. "THE DISPLACED PERSON"

By examining each of its six parts[24] individually, we can discuss the reasons "The Displaced Person" is one of O'Connor's most successful stories. Like most of her stories, the first part provides introductions. We meet the principal characters: Mrs. McIntyre, a sixty-year-old, once widowed, twice divorced; Mrs. Shortley, wife of the dairyman (Chauncey), fat, opinionated, bossy; the Guizacs, industrious displaced persons; the priest, an eighty-year-old eccentric; the peacock which fascinates the priest, is just another mouth to feed for Mrs. McIntyre, and is taken for granted by Mrs. Shortley; and the two Negroes, Astor the old man and the yellowish boy Sulk. O'Connor, incidentally, uses the peacock as a major symbol here for the first time, a symbol which she explains in a letter to Janet McKane: "The eyes in the tail stand for the eyes of the Church" (*HB*, p. 509). Twice mentioned, vision and eye glasses alert us to significant symbols and the idea of characters' varying abilities to see. Also in this section we are introduced to two important attitudes. Mrs. McIntyre feels that her help takes advantage of her; and Mrs. Shortley, who is very protective of her family, promotes dissension through gossip. Through her gossip we discover that the Shortley's feel their job security is threatened when the Guizacs arrive.

The second part begins three weeks later. The Displaced Person has proved his worth through industry and know-how. Mrs. McIntyre praises the Displaced Person and insinuates that the Shortleys do not save her money, one of her constant concerns. Mrs. Shortley's suspicion mounts; and after her comment about the "illogic of niggers," she twists the events to place the blame on the priest (and religion) as a threat to Astor and Sulk, for whom she is willing to take up. Chauncey shows up more as a henpecked husband, and Mrs. Shortley's ignorance also becomes more apparent: about Europe, about people, about religion.

In the third part Mrs. Shortley's furor, finally worked into a rage, culminates in her making her family leave the farm. On their way out Mrs. Shortley has another vision, one that puts her into a catatonic state. According to one critic, it is "the most clearly developed case of demonic revelation" in O'Connor's works.[25] Although some readers wince at the rather sudden disappearance of Mrs. Shortley half way through the story, we can see that O'Connor has shifted the conflict to Mrs. McIntyre and the Displaced Person. The problem can no longer be blamed on Mrs. Shortley, and Mrs. McIntyre's character is more clearly delineated. Underlying the issue of Mrs. McIntyre's soul, which O'Connor leaves in the capable hands of Father Flynn, is the question of racial and ethnic prejudices. Even "trash" like the Shortleys can consider themselves "above" blacks and foreigners. Who in this story leads the more exemplary life? In the end, the Displaced Person whom Mrs. McIntyre identifies with Christ.

The fourth part is complex. We gain some more background about Mrs. McIntyre's three husbands, the Displaced Person's plan is revealed by Sulk, and Mrs. McIntyre confronts the Displaced Person about his white cousin's coming to the United States to marry black Sulk. Again and again, money is the number one concern for Mrs. McIntyre. Ironically and erroneously, she tells Astor: " 'Money is the root of all evil' "; but in the Judge's room, a safe sits like a tabernacle. After her confrontation with the Displaced Person, Mrs. McIntyre mounts a hill to watch Guizac work; and she strikes a pose not unlike Mrs. Shortley's stance in the opening paragraph. Hence, we feel the tension and conflict shift and unify: Mrs. McIntyre versus "trash."

In the fifth part, Mrs. McIntyre tells the priest that the Displaced Person is "not working out" because he does not understand how to work with blacks. The priest, however, remains preoccupied with the peacocks and declares that Christ will come like the effect of the peacocks' tails, in a blaze of glory "to redeem us."

"Mrs. Shortley's mouth had drawn acidly to one side." ("The Displaced Person") Pictured is Shirley Stoller, who played Mrs. Shortley in The Displaced Person. *Photograph by Barbara McKenzie, reprinted by permission of Barbara McKenzie and* The Georgia Review.

A month has passed when the last part begins. Mr. Shortley returns and Mrs. McIntyre rehires him. She resolves to let the Displaced Person go although she is bothered by a "moral obligation." When Father Flynn returns to give Mrs. McIntyre more instruction, she declares, "Christ was just another Displaced Person!" Her argument is based on money. With that declaration and with her belief that the Displaced Person has upset the balance, we are reminded of the Misfit in "A Good Man Is Hard to Find." Mrs. McIntyre does not have the resolve necessary to fire the Displaced Person; she has never had to turn anyone out because they all just left her like the Shortleys did. Mr. Shortley, who has become more assertive since his wife died, stirs up sentiment against Mrs. McIntyre because she has allowed a "foreigner" to threaten their jobs. Thus Mrs. McIntyre's "moral obligation" to "her own" takes precedence over the priest's "moral obligation" to Mankind, to Christ. The description of the "accident" binds Mrs. McIntyre, Astor, and Mrs. Shortley as accomplices forever. No one even tries to help the Displaced Person. Their collusion fits that described by the Easterner in Stephen Crane's "The Blue Hotel": "We are all in it! . . . Every sin is the result of a collaboration." Like the gambler, the Displaced Person "came merely as a culmination, the apex if a human movement, and gets all the punishment."[26] Perhaps not all the punishment. The accident results in Mrs. McIntyre's decline in fiscal and physical state. Mr. Shortley and Sulk leave, and Astor is too old to work alone. She sells at a loss and eventually becomes bedridden. Her only companion is the priest who visits faithfully to instruct her in the teachings of the Church. Divine justice.

OTHER STORIES ABOUT RACE: "The Geranium," "The Artificial Nigger," "Everything That Rises Must Converge," and "Revelation."

13. "A TEMPLE OF THE HOLY GHOST"

This story conjures wonderful associations of the sister's initiation in Katherine Anne Porter's story "The Grave," with the sun imagery in Stephen Crane's *The Red Badge of Courage,* and with the thematic thrusts of William Blake's "Tyger, Tyger" and Robert Frost's "Design."

"A Temple of the Holy Ghost" is about a twelve-year-old girl (unnamed) who is visited by two "second cousins" who attend the convent, both age fourteen. The fourteen-year-olds, Susan and Joanne, are typical teenage girls, boy-crazy and pretentiously wise in front of the "child." The child, though, is precocious and is, as she unfortunately realizes, smarter than her cousins. She helps her mother think of two boys, Wendell and Cory, who might entertain Susan and Joanne by taking them to the fair. It is arranged. The boys, who want to be Church of God preachers, try serenading the

Mrs. McIntyre "watched as he came out of the barn. . . ." ("The Displaced Person") Photograph by Charles S. Ford.

girls, who respond with the *Tantum Ergo*[27] as an end to the singing. When they return from the fair, the girls tell the child of a "freak," a hermaphrodite who shows its secret to the audience with the admonishment that if they laugh God might strike them that way.

That revelation has an effect on the child as does the expression "a temple of the Holy Ghost,"[28] which the girls titteringly use to describe their bodies. When the mother and child take the cousins back to the convent, they attend mass. During the Eucharist the child feels the presence of God, and she prays that she will not be so sarcastic and ugly to people.

The story, then, is an initiation of the child of pride into a secular reality of the world (the hermaphrodite) and into the spiritual reality of Christ. It is the child's story; the other characters' actions simply deny or confirm her observations and conclusions: about the relationship between Mrs. Kirby and Mr. Cheatam; about Alonzo Myers, the taxi driver who reminds her of a pig; about the two teenage couples; about the fair and her fantasies; about the freak; and about the Eucharist. Her epiphany seems complete.

OTHER STORIES ABOUT CHILDREN: "The Turkey," "The River," "A Circle in the Fire," "The Artificial Nigger," "A View of the Woods," "The Lame Shall Enter First," and *The Violent Bear It Away*.

14. "THE ARTIFICIAL NIGGER"

According to O'Connor, "The Artificial Nigger" is her favorite and best written story (*HB* p. 209). About how it came to be written, Mary Barbara Tate relates this anecdote: On a trip to a neighboring town, Flannery saw a statue of an "artificial nigger" in a yard near her destination. She said then that she was going to write a story about it. And she did.

It is a story of youth, age, and redemption. Mr. Head's idea is "that only with years does a man enter into that calm understanding of life that makes him a suitable guide for the young." Coming at the beginning of the story, his idea is ironic; but it sets up the journey motif which hints of other, more famous journeys and guides—Virgil and Dante, Raphael and Tobias. Mr. Head is his grandson's guide in the city.[29]

The purpose of the trip is to teach Nelson a moral lesson on the sin of pride. But we soon wonder who is more guilty of that sin. Their closeness in sharing that guilt even manifests itself in the fact that they look more like brothers than grandfather and grandson. O'Connor's imagery forebodes the disaster of the trip: the moon, the grayness they face, the apparition (train) which is to take them, the sleeping bodies askew in the train car, their reflections as ghosts on the windows, the pimp and his two whores, and their leaving their lunch on the train—all ominous omens.

After they arrive in the city, Mr. Head's lack of knowledge becomes more apparent. He explains the sewer system as a descent into hell, and he keeps them walking in circles to avoid getting lost. When they turn into a black neighborhood, they encounter a woman with a knowing expression, a "fierce-looking boy on a bicycle," "black eyes in black faces" watching them, a big black woman in a pink dress to whom Nelson is inexplicably attracted. Mystery is all around them. Later when Mr. Head's lesson for Nelson backfires and Nelson bolts into another pedestrian, Mr. Head denies knowing the boy. Mr. Head subsequently abandons hope as their journey takes them through alternating hot-cold imagery.

Their trials along the way lead Mr. Head to a moment of illumination. He understands how man would be without hope of salvation. Upon entering another neighborhood they see a statue of an "artificial nigger" which serves as the catalyst and reunites them "like an action of mercy." Mr. Head then gains his knowledge of mercy through the agony of sin. O'Connor explains her intention in a letter to Ben Griffith: "What I had in mind to suggest with the artificial nigger was the redemptive quality of the Negro's suffering for us all" (*HB*, p. 78).

OTHER STORIES ABOUT YOUTH AND AGE: "Wildcat," "A Late Encounter with the Enemy," "A View of the Woods," and *The Violent Bear It Away*.

15. "GOOD COUNTRY PEOPLE"

"Good Country People" focuses on Joy (Hulga), Mrs. Hopewell's crippled daughter of thirty-two years and a Ph.D. Hulga, her self-chosen name with all the pejorative associations (hull = hulk = huge = ugly), grows more like herself, "bloated, rude, and squint-eyed." Her belief in nothing is based on Martin Heidegger's writings, and her studies encompass the French philosopher Nicolas Malebranche, who correlated sensation with mental creation to correspond with things in the physical creation.[30] Her defense mechanism for her wooden being is intellectualism. Mrs. Hopewell is one of those O'Connor characters who "had no bad qualities of her own but [who] was able to use other people's in such a constructive way that she never felt the lack." Her sayings, "nothing is perfect," "that is life," and "other people have their opinions too," reflect her eternal optimism and complete lack of understanding. Mrs. Freeman, another stock character, is her opposite. Manley Pointer is the Bible salesman with whom Hulga becomes involved, and Mrs. Freeman's daughters are foils to Hulga who after all is not so unlike them.

Hulga agrees to meet Manley Pointer, and they go for a walk. She imagines herself seducing him and even lets him kiss her, an "unexceptional experience" controlled by the mind (Malebranche's theory), she reasons.

"It was not possible to tell if the artificial Negro were meant to be young or old. . . ." ("The Artificial Nigger")
Photograph by Barbara McKenzie, reprinted by permission of Barbara McKenzie and
The Georgia Review.

They arrive at a hay barn and go in, at which point Manley produces a false bible, hollow inside and filled with a pocket flask of whiskey, a deck of dirty-picture cards, and a box of condoms. Hulga says to him that seeing nothing is "a kind of salvation," but she is "as sensitive about the artificial leg as a peacock about his tail." Without her leg, she becomes dependent on him, whom she sees as complete innocence. Hulga is defiled by Manley Pointer without his completing the seduction: he takes her glasses and her leg and brags to her that he once got a woman's glass eye the same way. He in fact is not innocent and tells her he has been believing in nothing ever since he was born. Hulga is a maimed soul, maimed.[31]

Mrs. Freeman's last statement sums up the relationships among these "good country people": "Some can't be that simple . . . I know I never could." It suggests that she has seen through Manley Pointer's deceit and Mrs. Hopewell has not.

OTHER STORIES WITH EXISTENTIAL OVERTONES: "A Good Man Is Hard to Find," "The Life You Save May Be Your Own," "The Enduring Chill," "The Partridge Festival," and *The Violent Bear It Away*.

16. "GREENLEAF"

"Greenleaf" contains overt religious symbolism and an abundance of metaphors: for the former, the bull, a crown of thorns, circles, the trinity, a chalice, the names Wesley and Scofield, the number seven, the use of prayer-healing, an image of a snake, the word "Jesus," references to lilies, the devil, and judgment; for the latter, "like some patient god come down to woo her," "like an uncouth country suitor," "like a menacing prickly crown," "like the crest of some disturbed bird," "like a rough chalice," "stiff as a rake handle," "as composed as a bulldog's" expression, "like other words inside the bedroom," "like a silver bullet," "like a knife edge," "like an old horse," "like a large bug," and "like a wild tormented lover." In using figures of speech that play religion off against nature, O'Connor combines two forces which she says are inseparable to emphasize her theme of redemption.

The story has three discernible parts. It opens with Mrs. May's being awakened by a bull that has broken loose from its pen. The loose bull gives cause for her to reflect on her tenant farmhands, the Greenleafs, and specifically on Mr. Greenleaf. From her interior monologue, we learn about Mrs. May's character; she is opinionated, proud, and self-pitying.

The basis of the real conflict emerges in the second part. The Greenleaf's sons, O. T. and E. T., have done well; they were sergeants in the war, married French women, went to college, built a brick duplex, and now farm. Mrs. May's two sons, Wesley and Scofield, are at best not worth shooting: they live with their mother, sass and make fun of her, do not help her farm, and are indifferent toward her problems. Scofield is a "policy man," an insurance salesman for blacks; and Wesley is an "intellectual," a teacher who hates everything. Mrs. Greenleaf is a prayer-healer who wallows in the dirt over miseries of people she does not even know, a lazy person in Mrs. May's eyes. When Mrs. May learns that the loose bull belongs to O. T. and E. T., she has a tantrum and rails to Mr. Greenleaf about his sons' lack of responsibility. The scene ends with Mrs. May's threat that she will have Mr. Greenleaf shoot the bull if the bull is not removed from her property.

Violence dominates the third part of the story. There is a sense of violent awe when Mrs. May drives to the Greenleaf boys' farm to deliver her ultimatum about their bull. To her horror, she discovers a sense of pride and cleanliness about their place. Inside, their dairy barn sparkles with a blinding brilliance. Juxtaposed to that discovery is the messiness of her own sons, who when she returns home bait and insult her. In a rage she orders Mr. Greenleaf to shoot the bull, and the bull again gets loose. The next morning she and Mr. Greenleaf drive to the pasture to kill the bull. She parks in the center of the pasture to wait, becomes impatient, and honks her horn— a noise which infuriates the bull. He charges and gores her through her heart. Mr. Greenleaf completes the violent scene by shooting the bull.

The religious symbolism which has accompanied the violent crescendo raises in our minds the question of redemption: Does Mrs. May accept her moment of grace? How do we read the line, "she had the look of a person whose sight has been suddenly restored but who finds the light unbearable"? That she can "see" again (or really for the first time) may be a revelation, but the fact that the vision is "unbearable" seems ambiguous. Because of the force of the revelation, is it too overwhelming for her to take in all at once? Or, because of the magnitude of her sins, of which she has been unaware, can she not accept the truth of the revelation? The reality of the situation offers Mrs. May a basis for understanding, but textually, as John R. May points out, we find little evidence that she accepts or rejects that offer.[32] She only seems to be "whispering some last discovery into the animal's ear," the narrator of the story tells us. Perhaps in the last analysis we are at least comforted by the fact that her moment came, regardless of her choice, because in believing that we can share in the faith that our moment will also come, even in an unexpected and violent way.

OTHER STORIES ABOUT MOTHER-SON RELATIONSHIPS: "A Good Man Is Hard to Find," "The River," "The Enduring Chill," "The Comforts of Home," and "Everything That Rises Must Converge."

17. "A VIEW OF THE WOODS"

O'Connor's "little morality play," "A View of the Woods" portrays the sin of Pride manifested in a grandfather, Mr. Fortune, and his nine-year-old

Mrs. May "opened the milking room door and stuck her head in and for the first second she felt as if she were going to lose her breath." ("Greenleaf")
Photograph by Charles S. Ford

granddaughter, Mary Fortune Pitts. Mr. Fortune tries to rear and train his granddaughter to be a FORTUNE (materialist) rather than a PITTS (naturalist). He spends his time with her, gives her gifts which she does not ask for, and hints that she will inherit his land and money when he dies. Mr. Fortune envisions himself as a man of progress; he sells part of his 800 acres, a lot at a time, in hopes that the area around the lake will develop and that a town (Fortune) will spring up. He is also vindictive. He allows his daughter, son-in-law, and their seven children to live on his land and to make their living from it, but he maintains control over everything. The conflict arises when he decides to sell a strip of land between their house and the road, affectionately called "the lawn" by the Pittses. Mary Fortune gives him three sound reasons why he should not sell it: it will spoil their view of the woods, her daddy grazes calves on it, and it is where the children play. Unmoved, the grandfather sells to Tilman, a hustler who has devilish characteristics of a snake.

Mary Fortune, described as her grandfather's image, rejects Mr. Fortune when he sells the land. Mr. Fortune concludes that he has spoiled her by not being "tougher" with her, and he tries to spank her. She proudly informs him, "Nobody's ever beat me in my life and if anybody did, I'd kill him." They fight, and in fact she does kill him (heart condition). Before his stroke, however, she hits her head on a rock (an accident) and dies.

This macabre ending is laced with imagery to suggest the inner turmoil of Mr. Fortune, a turmoil heightened in his mind because he sees in a mysterious way that Mary Fortune is his other self. The machine-in-the-garden imagery, that is, the bulldozer which he has helped bring into the garden, hints at his materialistic view of life and provides a secular motif; the woods, about which he has nightmares, offer the contrasting view of nature and a religious motif.

On another level this story is about familial love, which Mr. Fortune cannot give. His love is for money and power, which he sees continuing in Mary Fortune. Mary Fortune, he decides, respects her father because he spanks her and enforces discipline. Besides the grandfather-granddaughter relationship, O'Connor has two father-daughter relationships at work: Mr. Fortune and his daughter, Pitts and Mary Fortune. Which one works best? Apparently O'Connor is saying the later one, which does not break the old adage "spare the rod, spoil the child," is more meaningful.

Mary Fortune's loyalty to Pitts is her "flaw," an ugly mystery to Mr. Fortune. Another mystery, uncomfortable to him, is the woods. In his final vision of the woods and the lake just before he dies, that mystery is partially revealed through the gaunt trees thickening into "mysterious dark files that were marching across the water and away into the distance." In her essay "Catholic Novelists and Their Readers," O'Connor writes that the Christian storyteller "is like the blind man whom Christ touched, who looked then and saw men as if they were trees, but walking" (*MM*, p. 184). In that way is Mr. Fortune touched.

The last thing he sees, however, is the bulldozer; but the mechanical monster cannot help him. Nature is indifferent to him, and he rejects salvation (the woods as Christ symbol).[33]

OTHER STORIES ABOUT MATERIALISM: "The Life You Save May Be Your Own," "The Displaced Person," "Greenleaf," and *Wise Blood*.

18. "THE ENDURING CHILL"

"The Enduring Chill" is yet another story with a three-part structure. In the first part, Asbury Fox returns from New York City to his home, Timberboro, Georgia. Asbury, age twenty-five, an indulged boy with an "artistic temperament," comes home to die, he thinks. His mother Mrs. Fox, age sixty, and his sister Mary George, at age thirty-three principal of an elementary school, pick him up from the train and drive him to the house. During the ride he is impudent and surly; and in his somewhat distorted, romantic way, he relishes the thought of his dying as a sort of punishment on his family. His creative efforts have been a bust. His life, too. He thinks of two "friends" in New York: Goetz, a pseudomystic who defines salvation as "the destruction of a simple prejudice," and a priest, Ignatius Vogle, S.J., whom Asbury sees at a lecture on Vedānta.[34] His friends mirror the wide disparity between what Asbury wants to be and what he really is.

The middle part, transitional in nature, describes the afternoon of Asbury's first day home. Mrs. Fox summons Dr. Block in spite of Asbury's protests that his ailment is beyond Block's capabilities. Before Block, a stereotypical country doctor, leaves he takes a blood sample from Asbury.

The concluding part provides clues to and ultimately reveals Asbury's problem. Sitting on the porch, Asbury recalls the previous year when he had smoked in the milk barn and had drunk fresh, warm milk. Morgan and Randall, the black dairymen, smoked with him but would not drink the milk. Nor would they give him a reason for not drinking except to say, "She don't 'low it." After that flashback, Asbury badgers his mother into inviting a priest, rather than their Methodist minister Dr. Bush, to visit him. Father Finn from Purrgatory calls; he is "blind in one eye, deaf in one ear." Instead of discussing James Joyce, as Asbury had envisioned, Father Finn begins to instruct him and chides Asbury for not knowing his catechism. The scene is another direct attack on Asbury's dwindling self-esteem.

Asbury seeks "some last culminating experience" of his own doing (his sin of Pride), a wish granted with an ironic twist. Block discovers that Asbury has undulant fever from drinking the impure milk, a result of his own

doing. After that, Asbury recognizes that he will live "in the face of a puri-
fying terror." O'Connor explains that terror: Asbury "undeniably realizes
that he's going to live with the new knowledge that he knows nothing. That
really is what he is frozen in—humility" (*HB*, p. 261). His humility is fur-
thered by the water stain which symbolizes "the Holy Ghost, emblazoned in
ice instead of fire, [as it] continued, implacable, to descend" on Asbury.[35]

OTHER STORIES USING CLERGY: "The River," "The Displaced Person," "A Temple of the Holy Ghost," *Wise Blood*, and *The Violent Bear It
Away*.

19. "THE COMFORTS OF HOME"

Given Thomas's attachment to his electric blanket, the word "comforts"
in the title takes on a double meaning which adds to the humor of this other-
wise gruesome story.

Thomas, a typical male chauvinist, sees virtue as a principle of order, but
the virtues he approves of in his mother are a tidy house and good meals.
His mother's capacity for charity is enormous even though she herself seems
a bit naive. She takes in a nymphomaniac, alias Star, age nineteen, who has
been arrested for passing bad checks. Thomas describes Star as a "shrewd
ragamuffin." Through the word "shrewd," O'Connor introduces the idea of
an evil, malevolent force. Thomas is bothered by his mother's
"engagements with the devil," whom he says she would never recognize.

Thomas writes history, a vocation which should give him a perspective
on mankind. Not so. His confrontations with Sarah (Star) are less than
satisfactory; he cannot articulate his thoughts, and she just laughs, a
bodiless laugh, at him. Thomas's rage grows. The ghost of Thomas's father
appears to him, and Thomas is caught in a tug-of-war between his mother
and his dead father, between Christian charity and pragmatic action.
Thomas's "plan for all practical action [is] to wait and see what develop[s]."
His father's urgings prompt him to go to Sheriff Farebrother after Thomas
discovers that his gun is missing. They devise a scheme through which the
sheriff will find the gun in Sarah's possession. When Thomas finds the gun
back in his desk moments before the sheriff is to arrive, he tries to slip it into
Sarah's purse; but she catches him. He damns the order of the universe
(therefore, for him, virtue too) for creating Sarah Ham. Thomas grabs the
gun, his mother intervenes just as Thomas pulls the trigger: matricide. The
sheriff enters in time to draw his own conclusion—the "lovers" getting rid of
"extra baggage." It is an O. Henry ending.

Is the voice of the father, an admittedly evil man, that of the devil? If so,
he uses Thomas, an unwitting soul that cannot act, as his means of
vengeance; and Sarah becomes the devil's assistant. The situation reverses

the notion that good can come out of evil; in this story, out of good (the mother) comes bad.

OTHER STORIES TOUCHING THE CRIMINAL ELEMENT: "A Good Man Is Hard to Find," "The Life You Save May Be Your Own," "The Partridge Festival," and "The Lame Shall Enter First."

20. "EVERYTHING THAT RISES MUST CONVERGE"[36]

Douglas Rhymes suggests we need to recognize that

we are simply us in all our rages, the Rogues' Gallery of humanity, not the Royal Academy of Saints, and yet in just that moment when we know our acceptance we are also the Royal Academy of Saints.[37]

"Everything That Rises Must Converge" is a story which illustrates Rhymes's point. Julian, the martyr, shows a loss of faith; but his mother has tremendous "faith" and comfort in knowing who she is, an ironic statement in light of their somewhat impoverished situation. She lives with memories of her past and their ancestry who "were someone." While waiting on the bus which will take her to her "free" weight-reducing class, Julian has an "evil urge to break her spirit," an urge which proves to be a reality.

They argue about "true culture" which for Julian is only in the mind; for his mother, it is in the heart. The heart, however, as O'Connor would know from Joseph Conrad and Nathaniel Hawthorne, has its dark corners. Julian's mother utters the typical segregationist statements which embarrass Julian, but what Julian resents most in his mother is her not knowing who she is (at least from his perspective). His self-analysis of his being free from his mother is of course not true. After the push-and-pull between Julian and his mother, a big black woman with her four-year-old son boards the bus. She is wearing a hat identical to the one Julian's mother is wearing. Besides prompting internal reaction of Julian's mother to the black woman, the incident motivates the action that follows. Coincidentally, they get off at the same stop, and when Julian's mother tries to give the little boy a penny, the child's mother hits Julian's mother with her purse and stuns her. Julian tries to reinforce the "lesson" by explaining that the old world to which his mother clings is gone. The blow does damage, though, and Julian's mother passes out looking at him first and finding nothing. She is momentarily part of that Royal Academy of Saints; and he, part of the Rogues' Gallery as he is about to enter the world of guilt and sorrow.

Sister Feeley contends that this story unites O'Connor's ideas about "personal integrity, man's relationship with society, and the power of death to give life new clarity."[38] The story also seems to suggest a weakness in people who cling to the past blindly, without attempting to adapt to the present and to look toward the future.

OTHER STORIES ABOUT SELF-KNOWLEDGE: "The Geranium," "The Artificial Nigger," "Greenleaf," "The Comforts of Home," "The Partridge Festival," "Revelation," and *Wise Blood*.

21. "THE PARTRIDGE FESTIVAL"

Partridge is the town; azalea, the festival. Calhoun, twenty-three and great-nephew of Aunts Bessie and Mattie, visits Partridge ostensibly to see the azalea festival, but actually to learn more about a man named Singleton, who having endured mock arrest for not wearing an Azalea Festival Badge, shot and killed six citizens of that community. The festival goes on as normal, however. Calhoun, the narrator reveals, is like Singleton inside.[39]

Calhoun, a writer, has come to do an exposé on Singleton and subconsciously to mitigate his own guilt feelings. In the city he sells refrigerators, air coolers, and boats in the summer and shares a flat with two other boys in the winter. At selling, he excels. That fact is contrary to his philosophical bent toward existentialism, on which he expounds to Mary Elizabeth: "I mean your existential encounter with his [Singleton's] personality. The mystery of personality . . . is what interests the artist. Life does not abide abstractions." Mary Elizabeth, the aunts' neighbor, harbors a similar resentment about the festival and claims to be a journalist/novelist. They find a common ground in Singleton.

Calhoun and Mary Elizabeth alienate themselves from their community through their self-righteous judgments. We meet some of that community through Calhoun who tries to "interview" people about the murders: a soda jerk, the old man in the hardware store, a "small white girl," and the barber. The barber, it turns out, is "related" to Singleton via his second cousin who married Singleton's sister-in-law. From the barber's rendition of the incident and from the people Calhoun meets, we feel a sense of community not unlike that portrayed in Faulkner's *Light in August*. Singleton is outside Partridge the same way Joe Christmas is outside Jefferson but without the racial implications. The community of Partridge is a group of people who are "tied together by bonds that make them one cohesive group,"[40] a realization both Calhoun and Mary Elizabeth eventually come to accept.

Before they reach that conclusion, Mary Elizabeth refers to Singleton as a Christ-figure and Calhoun sees him as salvation. Somewhere, Calhoun feels, a revelation is at hand. Indeed it is. They drive to the asylum where Singleton is being held and pose as relatives in order to see him. Confronted by a spider-like creature with reptilian eyes, they flee in fright when

Singleton exposes (reveals) his naked self to Mary Elizabeth. Safe in their car, Calhoun sees the reflection of a "master salesman" mirrored in Mary Elizabeth's glasses. It is their discovery of self-knowledge. In a letter to John Hawkes, O'Connor observes the following about Singleton: "as he stands I look on him as another comic instance of the diabolical. . . . Fallen spirits are of course still spirits, and I suppose the Devil teaches most of the lessons that lead to self-knowledge . . ." (*HB*, p. 439).

OTHER STORIES ABOUT COMMUNITY: "The Barber," "The Artificial Nigger," "Everything That Rises Must Converge," "Revelation," "Judgement Day," and *The Violent Bear It Away*. Of course, all O'Connor's stories deal with segments of a community; but it is interesting to note that we usually realize a stronger sense of community when her characters are somewhat separated from it or when they are in the larger context of a city.

22. "THE LAME SHALL ENTER FIRST"

From the first paragraph, the reader has a hint of one of the controlling themes in this story: alienation. Norton, the ten-year-old son, is alienated from his father, Sheppard, because Sheppard (shepherd of what?), a city recreational director who takes in Rufus Johnson from the reform school, poses an implicit threat to Norton, who is dominated by selfishness.

Sheppard is fascinated with the "space age" and mechanical things, that is, with technology. He is not a religious man, and he ignores Rufus's response that "the Devil made him [Rufus] do" those mischievous things. The telescope Sheppard buys for Rufus becomes a symbol, an instrument with which one sees more clearly. That Sheppard does not see more clearly is heightened irony.

Rufus gains an unexpectedly firm control over Norton after their first meeting. Rufus orders Norton around and explores the house at will, with Norton in tow. Sheppard fails to recognize the power Rufus is gaining over his son; he regards Rufus as a defective mechanism, something that can be repaired. When Rufus agrees to stay with Sheppard, Norton behaves badly and Sheppard whips him. Rufus, on the other hand, is allowed free rein: he defiantly sleeps in the mother's bedroom, a shrine to her memory. Rufus introduces Norton to the idea of Heaven and Hell, but with more emphasis on Hell, evil, and death. Norton responds to Rufus's attention with questions which Sheppard is oblivious to. Rufus, with Satanic characteristics—a hiss in his voice, a knotted face—talks of Hell as if he has some personal knowledge of it.

Sheppard then betrays Rufus when he is first accused of vandalism; but the second time he backs Rufus and denies Norton, who asks for him. Rufus spitefully rejects the new shoe (help) that Sheppard has specially made for his clubfoot. Undaunted, Sheppard vouches again for Rufus when the police confront him. Rufus later confesses to Sheppard.

Rufus remains alienated from everyone; Sheppard, from Norton. The alienation theme works for the dichotomy between science and religion,[41] which O'Connor introduces through symbols. Rufus, who is evil, brings Norton to the Bible; their relationship wanes, however, as Norton becomes interested in the telescope (science). When Sheppard completely shuts out Norton in order to win Rufus's confidence, Norton suffers a loss of faith that leads to despair and ultimately to his attempting through suicide to join his dead mother in "heaven" among the stars. Sheppard realizes too late his own selfishness and his love for Norton. Sheppard does not know, nor does he listen to the truth Rufus cites: that only Jesus can save him.[42] He is in the end the most alienated character in the story, alienated from Christ. He represents, according to O'Connor, "the empty man who fills up his emptiness with good works" (*HB*, p. 491).

OTHER STORIES ABOUT ALIENATION: "The Geranium," "The River," "The Displaced Person," "The Artificial Nigger," "A View of the Woods," "The Partridge Festival," "Why Do the Heathen Rage?," and *The Violent Bear It Away*.

23. "WHY DO THE HEATHEN RAGE?"

"Why Do the Heathen Rage?" has been treated like a story in *The Complete Stories*, and it appeared in *Esquire* as an excerpt from a novel in progress. O'Connor's third novel was never finished. The circumstances and characters in this story are reminiscent of "The Enduring Chill."[43] The title comes from Psalm 2:1 (also Acts 4:25): "Why do the heathen rage, and the people imagine a vain thing?" Intellectualism—this time of Walter, the twenty-eight-year-old son—again appears to be the vanity involved.

Walter's father, Tilman, returns home after his stroke. His daughter Mary Maud, a schoolteacher, orders Walter to get up and open the door. After the stretcher bearing Tilman is inside, Walter's mother tells him to shut the door. And as he is being carried in, "Tilman's enraged left eye appeared to include [Walter] in its vision but he gave him no sign of recognition." Through such action and description, we realize how indifferent Walter really is. He lacks all conviction, we are told, of sin or election. He reads (a technique O'Connor uses in "Good Country People" to introduce a related subject) Saint Jerome; and it is after his mother reads an excerpt from Walter's book that she becomes aware that religion can be violent, too. Although O'Connor's brief comments about this story in her letters reveal her emphasis on Walter, as the "story" stands Mrs. Tilman's discovery dominates.

OTHER STORIES USING CLERGY: "The River," "The Displaced Person," "A Temple of the Holy Ghost," *Wise Blood*, and *The Violent Bear It Away*.

24. "REVELATION"

Like "Everything That Rises Must Converge," "Revelation" uses a cross section of society to help reveal the main character's personality. Twelve (a symbolic number, though perhaps unintentional) characters are described: Mrs. Turpin (protagonist), her husband Claud, the little blond child, the lean stringy old fellow, a well-dressed, gray-haired lady, the nurse, a secretary, the woman beside Claud, a fat teenage girl, a leathery old woman, a woman in a yellow sweatshirt, a redhead named Miss Finley, and the black delivery boy.

From this gathering in a physician's waiting room, we discover that Mrs. Turpin has a preferential hierarchy of people: the rich, home-and-land owners, just home-owners, white trash, and blacks. Basically, it is an economic hierarchy. Mrs. Turpin is, of course, thankful to be on the upper end.[44] As she is rejoicing to herself that things (her station in life) are not different, the fat teenager named Mary (virgin) Grace (redemption) hits Mrs. Turpin with a book and attacks her. Then Mary Grace calls her an "old wart hog." Stunned, Mrs. Turpin and Claud return home, and she confesses to her black workers what Mary Grace has called her. Afterwards she goes alone to the pig parlor where she defends herself to invisible guests, like the comforters of Job. Next she questions God and has a vision that, in essence, "the first shall be last and the last, first." O'Connor refers to her as a "country female Jacob. And [her] vision is purgatorial" (*HB*, p. 577). We have met Mrs. Turpin before: Julian's mother, Mrs. Tilman, Mrs. Hopewell, to name just three examples. Besides the hypocrisy that Mrs. Turpin displays in the waiting room, she reveals an overwhelming pride in her position within the community and in relation to God. O'Connor has returned in this story to a more explicit statement on race as well. It is one of her few stories, moreover, in which both husband and wife are living, although we do not doubt that it is Mrs. Turpin's story.

OTHER STORIES ABOUT HYPOCRISY: "A Good Man Is Hard to Find," "The Displaced Person," "Greenleaf," "Everything That Rises Must Converge," "The Partridge Festival," and *Wise Blood*.

25. "PARKER'S BACK"

Caroline Gordon says of "Parker's Back" that it is "the dramatization of that particular heresy which denies Our Lord corporeal substance" (*CS*, p. xv). As a gift to his wife, Parker has a Byzantine Christ figure tatooed on his back. Parker's wife, however, identifies all of his tatoos, with which he has become dissatisfied, as the vanity of vanities (Ecclesiastes 1:2). But O'Connor notes that "Sarah Ruth was the heretic—the notion that you can worship in pure spirit" (*HB*, p. 594).

With that acknowledged, it seems the story is fairly straightforward, at least now so, after readers have been exposed to so many of her other stories. In the marital relationship, Sarah Ruth is much like Kate in *The Taming of the Shrew*, but Parker is not like Petruchio. Why he married her, Parker does not even know. She is "plain, plain," with sharp eyes befitting her sharp tongue and temper. Parker ponders his choice of a mate and decides, the narrator tells us, "it was himself he could not understand."

Parker appears to be the more fervent sinner of the pair: before the marriage, he blasphemed, he fornicated, he lied, he defiled his body with tatoos (vanity), he drank too much, he was proud, and he was given to sloth. His name, however, is ironic: Obadiah Elihue, who in the Bible is a comforter of Job. Parker tries to comfort Sarah Ruth without success. He becomes gloomier and finally thinks about having a religious tatoo etched on his back to please her. Before he decides definitely, he has an accident in which a tree catches on fire. The burning-bush vision changes his life, and he rushes to the artist for a religious tatoo. After he reviews a lengthy catalog of religious tatoos, he chooses the Byzantine Christ figure "with all-demanding eyes," eyes not unlike Sarah Ruth's eyes. Before Parker shows Sarah Ruth, he thrice denies that "he's gone and got religion." But he accepts his fate to obey the eyes and places his faith in Sarah Ruth's knowing what he should do.

Two ironic twists follow. First Sarah Ruth does not recognize the face and refers to it as "more trash"—the heresy Caroline Gordon refers to. Second, after turning his back on his mother and later on the navy, he accepts his responsibility toward his wife and she turns her back on him.

OTHER STORIES ABOUT MALE—FEMALE WORK RELATIONSHIPS: "The Life You Save May Be Your Own," "The Displaced Person," and "Greenleaf."

THE NOVELS

Two novels—*Wise Blood* (1952), her first published book, and *The Violent Bear It Away* (1960)—comprise O'Connor's longer fiction. Novella might be a more accurate term because both books are in fact long short stories or short novels.[45] Their brief length does not diminish their quality, although most critics have found them less well wrought than O'Connor's short stories. O'Connor, however, has remained in them true to her vision and has developed in her novellas two memorable characters: Hazel Motes in *Wise Blood* and Francis Marion Tarwater in *The Violent Bear It Away*. In examining both works, we shall follow the procedure used with the short stories, that is, a careful look at these stories in relation to O'Connor's other fiction, her essays, and her letters.

WISE BLOOD

Although four of *Wise Blood*'s fourteen chapters were first published as short stories and appear in *The Complete Stories*, this novella forms a complete narrative in much the same way that *Go Down, Moses* does in its dealings with a single community. In the "Author's Note to the Second Edition," O'Connor tells us that "it is a comic novel about a Christian *malgré lui* [in spite of himself] . . . [and] free will does not mean one will, but many wills conflicting in one man. Freedom cannot be conceived simply. It is a mystery and one that a novel, even a comic novel, can only be asked to deepen."[46] The "one man" is Hazel Motes of Eastrod, Tennessee. His story moves from his attempt to free himself of his religious fundamentalist upbringing toward what he has known since age twelve: "that he was going to be a preacher." After a four-year stint in the army, Haze returns home and finds no more Moteses. Eastrod has become a ghost town. He travels to Taulkinham and falls under the spell of Asa Hawks, a "blind" preacher and his daughter Sabbath Lily. In fighting against his destiny to become a preacher, he founds "The Church Without Christ." Enoch Emery, a pathetically lonely youth of the city, befriends Haze, becomes his sole disciple, and furnishes Haze a surrogate "Christ-child" (new jesus), a shrunken man which he steals from the museum in the park. Enoch's role as prophet over, he dons a gorilla costume and is last heard of, the happiest "gorilla" in existence as if his "god had finally rewarded it," overlooking the city. "And Enoch walked with God, and he *was* not, for God took him" (Genesis 5:24). Another street preacher, Onnie Jay Holy, alias Hoover Shoats, attempts to join forces with Haze in order to work the crowds better. Haze rejects Holy's sham, discovers the truth about Asa Hawks, and moves closer toward acceptance of his own redemption and guilt.

The heavy emphasis on nothingness in chapter 1 reminds us of Hulga in "Good Country People" and suggests the Kierkegaardian "leveling" of man into society, into a sort of brave new world. The existentialist needs identity which he can gain through self-knowledge; self-knowledge, in turn, can create an openness with others and hence with God, an openness which leads to salvation. Haze resists, at first, that progression in his life; he tries to control his own life: for example, he plans to be in the army only four months, tries to return home, expects to avoid Jesus by avoiding sin, buys a car to escape, and so forth. All attempts fail, however. Even on the train to

Taulkinham, his upper berth (play on the word "birth") is like a coffin, suggesting his life-in-death dilemma.

Haze cannot avoid Jesus. With his preacher-grandfather's words echoing in his memory—"Jesus would have him [the sinner] in the end!"—Haze visits Miss Lenora Watts, a prostitute whose name he takes from a public restroom wall. To the cabby who drives him to Miss Watt's house, he says, "I ain't any preacher." A prophetic denial. He follows Asa Hawks who himself is feigning blindness in order to hawk his pamphlets on the streets. Haze does finally seduce (or is seduced by) Sabbath in an affair that ends in further emptiness for him. Finally, Haze confronts his other self, Shoat's hired prophet Solace Layfield, and kills him in an act of merciless brutality similar to that of the rookie policeman who later kills Haze "with his new billy." Haze's act, though, has been seen—and I agree—as the turning point for his own acceptance. In Solace's death, Haze as priest hears his last confession. Haze's self-inflicted expiation is his act of blinding himself with lime, in the same manner Asa Hawks reportedly was to have blinded himself.

Vision predominates in *Wise Blood*. Enoch, who supposedly possesses wise blood, senses in a "mystery beyond understanding" his role in Haze's church. That is one type of vision. Sight is another: Asa, the blind imposter, who is street-wise; Haze, who cannot see until he is physically blind (like Oedipus); and Mrs. Flood, Haze's landlady, who becomes absorbed in Haze's eyes "as if she had finally got to the beginning of something she couldn't begin." O'Connor offers sufficient support for this emphasis: Haze's name which suggests color and obscured vision plus "Motes" in connection with Matthew 7:3-5: "Why beholdest thou the mote that is in thy neighbor's eye, but considerest not the beam that is in thine own eye . . . thou hypocrite, first cast the beam out of thine own eye."[47] Haze's mother's glasses which he ironically keeps "in case his vision should ever become dim" and which he throws out the door of the room he and Sabbath cohabit. Eyes also reinforce the vision motif: Haze, Asa, Hoover Shoats, Enoch, Mrs. Flood—all have revealing eyes or take an unusual interest in eyes.

The movement of the story is toward Haze's conversion; the tension develops through Haze's inner conflict. He goes from the train and his encounter with Mrs. Wally Bee Hitchcock to an automobile, "a high rat-colored machine with large thin wheels and bulging headlights." O'Connor says about his car that it is "his pulpit and his coffin as well as something he thinks of as a means of escape . . . a kind of death-in-life symbol, as his blindness is a life-in-death symbol" (*MM*, p. 72). After his car is destroyed by the patrolman, Haze finds his means of escape and blinds himself. He becomes victim of Mrs. Flood's greed and ironically her guiding light toward salvation. He dies in a squad car, the victim of a rookie's insensitivity: the scene brings to mind General Sash's death on stage in "A Late Encounter with the Enemy."

THE VIOLENT BEAR IT AWAY

Francis Marion Tarwater, another Christian *malgré lui*, has combined qualities of Hazel Motes and Enoch Emery in O'Connor's second novella, *The Violent Bear It Away*.[48] Like Haze's moment, Tarwater's redemption follows unexpected violence; his fate to preach seems predestined. Like Enoch's wise blood, Tarwater's "remembering is done through the blood, it is a bequeathment, it takes account of what happens before a man is born as if he were there taking part. It is a physical absorption through the living body, it is a spiritual heritage. It is also a life's work."[49] Tarwater, reared by his great-uncle "to expect the Lord's call himself," receives it after encounters with the Devil, his trials in the city, and finally his burning-bush vision.

O'Connor begins her three-part novella, in one sense, at the end, that is, with Mason Tarwater's death; and she ends it at the beginning, that is, with Francis Marion Tarwater's rebirth into the life of a prophet. In an unpublished letter dated 5 August 1959 to the Brainard Cheneys, O'Connor explains that she is more concerned with prophecy in general than with accurate predictions.[50] About Mason's role, she writes: "[Readers] forget that the old man has taught [Tarwater] the truth and that now he's doing what is right, however crazy" (*HB*, p. 536). And in yet another letter, "[Mason] is very obviously not a Southern Baptist, but an independent, a prophet in the true sense. The true prophet is inspired by the Holy Ghost, not necessarily by the dominant religion of his region" (*HB*, p. 407).

Rayber, the schoolteacher and Tarwater's uncle, offers the tension necessary for conflict in the story. His dim-witted son, Bishop, is the catalyst. Because of Mason's attempts to make his nephew Rayber[51] a prophet, Rayber becomes embittered; and subsequently, after escaping Mason's clutches, he rejects religion and becomes a schoolteacher. (O'Connor has portrayed other "intellectuals" as refugees from God: Hulga in "Good Country People," Asbury in "The Enduring Chill," and Calhoun in "The Partridge Festival," for example.) Rayber then takes Francis Marion as his charge after Rayber's parents and his sister (Tarwater's mother) "perish" to prevent, he says, Mason's ruining another child's life. Mason goes to live with Rayber to baptize, along with other motives, Tarwater. He succeeds. After Mason dies, Tarwater returns to the city to live with Rayber, who has an unbaptized, dim-witted son named Bishop. Tarwater's revelation there leaves him with the knowledge that he is expected to baptize Bishop. Thus ends part I.

Part II, the longest part, deals with Tarwater's life in the city, Rayber's own sense of guilt, Tarwater's "Friend," and Bishop's baptism. The sense of the city is comparable to what Mr. Head and Nelson encounter in "The Artificial Nigger": lonely, full of dangers, surrealistic. After hearing the child-evangelist, Lucette Carmody, Tarwater has a moment in which he would accept Rayber's instruction and love; but the moment is lost in Rayber's wrath and self-pity over his son's, and his, affliction. Bishop is in many ways Rayber's burden. Paradoxically, he is Tarwater's salvation.

The scene shifts in the second half of part II from the city to Cherokee Lodge, only thirty miles from Powderhead, Mason's home. Rayber has planned the outing to make Tarwater face "his problem." The trip does just that, but not exactly in terms Rayber has in mind. Tarwater accepts Rayber's peace offering—a corkscrew opener which could symbolize a form of temptation to open a bottle, the technological side of life, or an opening to a new way of life—dons the new clothes Rayber has provided, and baptizes/drowns Bishop.

Tarwater seems truly to be "the kind of boy . . . that the devil is always going to be offering to assist, to give [him] a smoke or a drink or a ride, and to ask [him his] bidnis." There are three, perhaps four, intended representations of the Devil during Tarwater's travels: Meeks, the copper flue salesman; the old-looking young stranger in the lavender and cream-colored car; the "Friend" who talks inside Tarwater's head; and possibly Rayber, who seems at times to mouth the "Friend's" sentiments.[52] Tarwater indeed accepts three rides after he leaves Powderhead, the last explicitly fulfills Mason's prophecy. After his rape, Tarwater starts a fire (an act of cleansing) and knows "that his destiny forced him on to a final revelation."

Fire is one of three dominant symbols in *The Violent Bear It Away*; water and bread are, according to O'Connor, the other two (*HB*, p. 387). The latter two suggest the sacraments of baptism and the eucharist. Baptism is clear enough since the novella's focus is on it. O'Connor elaborates, however:

The whole action of the novel is Tarwater's selfish will against all that the little lake (the baptismal font) and the bread stand for. . . . Water is a symbol of purification and fire is another. Water . . . is a symbol of the kind of purification that God gives irrespective of our efforts or worthiness, and fire is the kind of purification we bring on ourselves—as in Purgatory. It is our evil which is naturally burnt away when it comes anywhere near God (*HB*, p. 387).

Just as Mason learns by fire (*VBIA*, p. 5), so does Tarwater in his burning-bush vision (*VBIA*, p. 242). Before that conversion, food and water do not satisfy Tarwater's hunger and thirst.

Regarding O'Connor's dealings with the sacraments throughout her stories, this one may be the only story which touches in some way on all seven. Besides *baptism* and the *eucharist*, Tarwater hears Rayber's *confession* about his attempted murder of Bishop. The *matrimony* between Rayber and Bernice Bishop is recounted in part by Mason and in part by Rayber. Mason's teaching of Tarwater might be compared to a *confirmation* of Tarwater; and at the end when Tarwater smears "a handful of dirt off his great-uncle's grave" on his forehead, Tarwater seems to be taking his "*orders*" in a self-ordained priesthood. *Unction* seems implicitly hinted at in the scene between Tarwater and Bishop at Cherokee Lodge: first, as they are checking in, Tarwater is finally able to look into Bishop's eyes; second, his realization that he had baptized Bishop even as he drowned him serves as a healing of his sick soul.[53]

O'Connor blends well the imagery, characterization, setting, action, time, and overall form to support her theme in *The Violent Bear It Away*. Rayber's mechanically deterministic life, his final existential point of view, and Mason's role as prophet—the schism between technology (science) and religion—culminate in the conflict Tarwater faces. The epiphanic command which he receives while prostrate on Mason's grave: "GO WARN THE CHILDREN OF GOD OF THE TERRIBLE SPEED OF MERCY" resolves his conflict quite naturally for the context O'Connor has created. Tarwater follows, at last, Saint James's admonition (1:22): "Be ye doers of the word, and not hearers only, deceiving your own selves." And Flannery O'Connor follows it, too.

4

A Kaleidoscope of Characters

This catalogue, utilitarian in nature, provides students and other readers a ready reference to the 200 characters in Flannery O'Connor's published canon. Since this listing aims at aiding readers rather than substituting for the readings themselves, the identifications only briefly describe the characters' appearances, mannerisms, and singularly descriptive expressions—that is, those aspects which might jog memory.

Numerous divisions of O'Connor's characters present themselves: the "normal" characters and the freaks, those capable of Redemption and those incapable of Grace, believers and nonbelievers, the businessmen and the farmers, the country folk and the city dwellers, males and females, for example. Some of those classifications are inherent in the chosen method of presentation; others require a judgment which might best be reserved for the readers themselves. Therefore, to provide the necessary descriptions in a logical order and at the same time to preclude subjective interpretations which could be misleading, arrangement is alphabetical by surname (Motes, Hazel), by baptismal name (Bailey), by other given names ("John"), and by descriptive names (the barber). When necessary, names are cross-referred (Sarah Ruth Cates—Sarah Ruth Parker).

Major characters' names appear in bold face type; *minor characters'* names, in italics; and OTHER CHARACTERS' names, in small capital letters. "Other characters" include those whose "presence" may influence the action but who do not appear in the story, e.g., Mrs. Carson; or those characters present but without discernible influence, e.g., Sarah Mae Shortley.

The characters are catalogued from *Wise Blood* (*WB*), *The Violent Bear It Away* (*VBIA*), and *The Complete Stories* (by individual title). This catalogue does not attempt to list those names which appear in manuscript drafts and which do not reappear in O'Connor's published works, e.g., Rufus Florida Johnson.[1] Viewed in this manner, O'Connor's characters collectively produce a pattern within a multifarious society, a pattern in which the characters' manners form the design and in which O'Connor's readers can discover the mystery of design.

THE CHARACTERS

Artist, about twenty-eight years old, thin and bald, with a self-tattooed owl on his head for advertisement. Does the final tattoo on Parker's back—"the haloed head of a flat stern Byzantine Christ with all-demanding eyes." ("Parker's Back")

Harry Ashfield, also "Bevel," age four or five with long face and bulging chin, for whom Mrs. Connin babysits. His spiritual hunger causes him to look for the Kingdom of Christ in the river. ("The River")

Mr. Ashfield, Harry's father, insensitive or uncaring. ("The River")

Mrs. Ashfield, Harry's mother, a floozy in "black satin britches and barefoot sandals and red toenails"; who becomes incensed because some "dolt of a preacher" might have prayed for her "affliction" and baptized her son. ("The River")

Astor, the elder of two of Mrs. McIntyre's black helpers. ("The Displaced Person")

Bailey, balding only son of the Grandmother and father of three; "typical" in the sense that he sees the world only in realistic (mundane) terms; "didn't have a naturally sunny disposition"; from Atlanta; wears a yellow shirt with blue parrot design for the family weekend. ("A Good Man Is Hard to Find")

Bailey's Mother (the Grandmother), lives with Bailey and his family and keeps a cat named Pitty Sing. A selfish, hypocritical little old woman who sets herself up as a "gentile Southern lady"; she is the catalyst for the action in the story. ("A Good Man Is Hard to Find")

Bailey's Wife, a young woman whose "face was as broad and innocent as a cabbage"; the mother of three. ("A Good Man Is Hard to Find")

The Barber, whom Calhoun harangues over the murder which occurred before the Azalea Festival; kin by marriage to Singleton. ("The Partridge Festival")

BERTHA, does the dishes while Miss Willerton crumbs the table. ("The Crop")

Bernice Bishop, welfare woman who attempts with Rayber to take Francis Marion from his great uncle. Marries Rayber, has one child by him, deserts them, and returns to welfare work in Japan. (*VBIA*)

Aunt Bessie, one of Calhoun's great aunts, box-jawed, dead-white hair, who addresses Calhoun as "Baby Lamb" and who feels he had better get himself a girl. ("The Partridge Festival")

Bevel, see Harry Ashfield.

Doctor Block, Fox's doctor in Timberboro; "irresistible to children"; cures Asbury. ("The Enduring Chill")

BLOND CHILD, wearing a dirty blue romper suit, eyes idle, slumped on couch in the doctor's waiting room. ("Revelation")

Bobby Lee, companion of The Misfit; fat boy in black trousers and a red sweat shirt with a silver stallion embossed on the front of it. ("A Good Man Is Hard to Find")

Powell Boyd, about thirteen years old; father worked for Mrs. Cope; middle-sized, silver-rimmed spectacles, wears a sweat shirt with a destroyer on the front; sullen, destructive. ("A Circle in the Fire")

Mr. Bush, retired Methodist minister and rare-coin collector whom Mrs. Fox wants to invite to cheer up her ailing son, Asbury. ("The Enduring Chill")

Red Sammy Butts, fat man who owned the Tower, a filling station and dance hall just outside Timothy, Georgia; "his stomach hung over [his khaki trousers] like a sack of meal swaying under his shirt"; considered by Bailey's mother as "a good man." ("A Good Man Is Hard to Find")

Red Sammy's Wife, object of rudeness from June Star, Bailey's daughter, when she says of June Star, "Ain't she cute?" ("A Good Man Is Hard to Find")

Calhoun, a would-be-rebel-artist-mystic, whose great-grandfather initiated the Partridge Azalea Festival. At heart, a salesman who seeks the murderer Singleton to let him know someone "understands." ("The Partridge Festival")

CARAMEL, see Carramae Freeman.

Lucette Carmody, the eleven (or twelve)-year-old child witness in the church which Francis Marion visits. (*VBIA*)

Caroline, Julian's mother's nurse. ("Everything That Rises Must Converge")

Mrs. Carson, remembered by Old Dudley because she put a geranium in her window "back home." ("The Geranium")

Carver, son of the black woman—the "ponderous figure"—who wears the identical hat to Julian's mother's hat. ("Everything That Rises Must Converge")

Sarah Ruth Cates, Parker's wife: plain, skin as tight as an onion, sharp eyes, and gap-toothed; doesn't smoke, dip, drink, curse, or paint. Thinks churches idolatrous. ("Parker's Back")

MR. CHEATAM, Miss Kirby's bald admirer; a rich old farmer who drives a "fifteen-year-old baby-blue Pontiac." ("A Temple of the Holy Ghost")

Chestney, Julian's grandfather. ("Everything That Rises Must Converge")

J. C. Connin, one of three sons of Harry Ashfield's babysitter; he teases Harry at the pig pen. ("The River")

Mrs. Connin, Harry Ashfield's baby sitter; a shift worker who takes Harry to a healing and who refuses Mr. Ashfield's money when she returns his son. ("The River")

SARAH MILDRED CONNIN, Mrs. Connin's daughter (?) who greets Harry Ashfield in aluminum curlers. ("The River")

Sinclair Connin, brother of J. C. Connin (q.v.). ("The River")

Spivey Connin, another brother of J. C. Connin (q.v.). ("The River")

Mrs. Cope, "Small and trim, with a large round face and black eyes" and wears a sun hat still stiff and bright green; a worker who takes extreme pride in her possessions. ("A Circle in the Fire")

Sally Virginia Cope, Mrs. Cope's twelve-year-old daughter—pale, fat, with a frowning squint, has braces— who observes the action. ("A Circle in the Fire")

[*Cousin*], twelve-year-old second cousin of Joanne; considers her cousins "morons"; fat face, braces, and a vivid imagination. Decides at various times to be a doctor, an engineer, a saint. . . . "She was eaten up also with the sin of Pride, the worst one." ("A Temple of the Holy Ghost")

Lucynell Crater, widow of fifteen years, the size of a cedar post, who hires Mr. Shiftlet, a drifter ("The Life You Save May Be Your Own")

Lucynell Crater, daughter; a large girl, retarded, deaf, and nearly thirty years old. Marries Mr. Shiftlet. ("The Life You Save May Be Your Own")

MR. CROOMS, Mrs. McIntyre's second husband who resides in the State Asylum. ("The Displaced Person")

Culver, one of Mrs. Cope's black workers. ("A Circle in the Fire")

The Displaced Person, named Guizac, referred to as "Gobblehook" by Mrs. McIntyre and Mrs. Shortley. A Polish immigrant who was "short and a little sway-backed and wore gold-rimmed spectacles" and did not smoke; a capable farm hand who seemed to Mrs. McIntyre to be her "salvation." ("The Displaced Person")

Star Drake, nineteen-year-old girl with "wide apple cheeks and feline empty eyes," who invades Thomas's house and whom Thomas's mother calls a "nimpermaniac"; also, a "congenital liar" and suicidal. ("The Comforts of Home")

Driver, driver of the lavender and cream-colored car, a "pale, lean, old-looking young man with deep hollows under his cheekbones"; wears yellow hair under his "panama hat." Rapes Tarwater. (*VBIA*)

Old Dudley, widower who lives in a boarding house with his daughter and her family in New York City. To him, a neighbor's geranium represents his roots, his home in Georgia. ("The Geranium")

Old Dudley's Daughter, who feels that she is just doing "her duty" by taking in her father. Married with a sixteen-year-old son. ("The Geranium")

Old Dudley's Son-in-Law, "a queer one," who drives trucks and who doesn't have much to do with Old Dudley. ("The Geranium")

Enoch Emery, eighteen-year-old who "looked like a friendly hound dog with light mange"; attended Rodemill Boys' Bible Academy and works for the City of Taulkinham. A person of instinct, he is last seen wearing a gorilla suit. (*WB*)

Sheriff Farebrother, slightly stooped, dishonest figure: "another edition of Thomas's father" except for his checkered shirt and Texas hat. Hopes for the worst in situations. ("The Comforts of Home")

FAT LADY, who sits next to Claud in the doctor's waiting room and who must hoist herself out of the chair. ("Revelation")

MISS FINLEY, the gum chewer with red hair, rather youngish and wearing red high-heeled shoes. ("Revelation")

Father Finn, Jesuit priest from "Purrgatory": hearty voice, large red face, gray hair, blind in one eye, deaf in one ear. Visits Asbury, but does not want to discuss literary matters. ("The Enduring Chill")

Mrs. Flood, Hazel Motes's landlady who decides to marry Haze, who she feels has cheated her of something she cannot comprehend, i.e., the "pin point of light." (*WB*)

Father Flynn, "a long-legged black-suited old man with a white hat on and a collar that he wore backwards," who sees Christ in Mrs. McIntyre's peacocks and who "comforts" her after her health declines, by explaining the doctrines of the Church. ("The Displaced Peson")

Dr. Foley, who was "everything to the niggers." Buys the property that Tanner's cabin is on and offers Tanner an opportunity to run a still for him. ("Judgement Day")

Mr. Fortune, seventy-nine-year-old grandfather who accepts his granddaughter, Mary Fortune Pitts, as the only Pitts with any character. Spoils her and sells away the Pitts's view of the woods. ("A View of the Woods")

Asbury Porter Fox, twenty-five-year-old sickling with receding hairline and artistic temperament. Feels hampered by his upbringing, but returns home to die only to learn that he must accept his past and himself. ("The Enduring Chill")

Mary George Fox, Asbury's thirty-three-year-old sister who is principal of the country elementary school; unsympathetic to her brother's needs. ("The Enduring Chill")

Mrs. Fox, Asbury's mother, a practical woman who fails to understand her son's inner conflict; age sixty. ("The Enduring Chill")

CARRAMAE FREEMAN, "Caramel" to Joy; age fifteen, married to Lyman and expecting. ("Good Country People")

GLYNESE FREEMAN, Carramae's older sister; "Glycerin" to Joy; dating Harvey Hill who is in chiropractor school. ("Good Country People")

Mrs. Freeman, works for Mrs. Hopewell and never admits error; one of the "good country people." ("Good Country People")

Gabe, see Old Gabriel.

Old Gabriel, although blind, can smell the wildcat which, he believes, is on its way to visit him. ("Wildcat")

GARNER, rather than share in the chores, does the *Morning Press* crossword puzzle while Lucia and Bertha do the dishes. ("The Crop")

GEORGE, at Ashfield's party, the man who identifies the stolen book—*The Life of Jesus Christ for Readers Under Twelve*—as "valuable." ("The River")

GEORGE, one of the young blacks who hunt the wildcat. ("Wildcat")

HARTLEY GILFEET, "Little Mister Good Fortune" and the bane of Ruby's existence in the apartment building; he is the six-year-old boy on the fifth floor. ("A Stroke of Good Fortune")

Alice Gilhard, friend of Ruller's mother; talks to Ruller about the turkey he has captured. ("The Turkey")

Hetty Gilman, the old woman beggar, God's answer to Ruller's prayer. ("The Turkey")

GLYCERIN, see Glynese Freeman.

Gobblehook, see The Displaced Person.

GODHIGH, Julian's grandmother whose family was "in reduced circumstances." ("Everything That Rises Must Converge")

GOETZ, student of Oriental philosophy and religion, and a "friend" of Asbury Fox in New York City. ("The Enduring Chill")

MR. GOVISKY, presented General Sash with the Confederate uniform twelve years prior to the graduation exercises. ("A Late Encounter with the Enemy")

The Grandmother, see Bailey's Mother.

E. T. Greenleaf, one of the twins, slightly younger than Mrs. May's sons; long-legged, raw-boned, red-skinned; married a French girl during WW II, returned to school on the G. I. Bill, took a government loan to start his farm. ("Greenleaf")

Mr. Greenleaf, tenant farmer for Mrs. May for fifteen years; "walked with a high-shouldered creep and he never appeared to come directly forward"; face shaped like "a rough chalice." ("Greenleaf")

Mrs. Greenleaf, whom Mrs. May cannot abide; mother of five girls and two boys. She was "large and loose," a prayer healer, and like Mrs. Pritchard enjoyed the morbid. ("Greenleaf")

O. T. Greenleaf, other twin; consequently, see E. T. Greenleaf. ("Green-leaf")

GRISBY BOY, polio victim who reminded Old Dudley of Mrs. Carson's geranium which was put out every morning to sun. ("The Geranium")

Guizac, see The Displaced Person.

Mrs. Guizac, Polish wife of The Displaced Person; upon arrival at Mrs. McIntyre's farm, was dressed "in brown, shaped like a peanut." ("The Displaced Person")

Rudolph Guizac, the son, age twelve, who served as translator between The Displaced Person (his father) and Mrs. McIntyre. ("The Displaced Person")

Sledgewig Guizac, nine-year-old daughter of The Displaced Person. Her name sounded to Mrs. Shortley "like something you would name a bug, or vice versa." ("The Displaced Person")

W. T. Harper, one of the three boys who visits Mrs. Cope's farm. Age thirteen, penetrating stare, sullen, destructive. ("A Circle in the Fire")

Asa Hawks, "blind" preacher who reportedly put lime in his eyes to prove his Faith; to whom Hazel Motes feels drawn and, at the same time, repelled. (*WB*)

Sabbath Lily Hawks, "blind" preacher's daughter, a bastard child of fifteen years who seduces Hazel Motes and deserts him. (*WB*)

Mr. Head, age sixty and of strong character that does not allow him to depend on mechanical things: tube-like face, long rounded open jaw, long depressed nose; Nelson's grandfather. ("The Artificial Nigger")

HEZUH, the black whom, according to Nancy, the wildcat got by the throat. ("Wildcat")

Bill B. Hill, Ruby's husband, a "Florida man who sold Miracle Products." ("A Stroke of Good Fortune")

HARVEY HILL, dates Glynese Freeman and attends chiropractor school. ("Good Country People")

Ruby Hill, age thirty-four and pregnant. Visits a palmist to learn that her long illness will bring her "a stroke of good fortune," a prediction which she interprets to mean a place in a subdivision. ("A Stroke of Good Fortune")

Hiram, second companion of The Misfit; wears khaki pants and a blue-striped coat and a gray hat. ("A Good Man Is Hard to Find")

Miss Hitchcock, see Mrs. Wallace Ben Hosen.

SARAH LUCILE HITCHCOCK, Mrs. Hitchcock's married daughter in Florida. (*WB*)

Mrs. Wally Bee Hitchcock, neé Miss Weatherman, the fat woman with pear-shaped legs whom Hazel Motes meets on the train to Taulkinham. (*WB*)

Hitchhiker, runaway who insults Mr. Shiftlet. ("The Life You Save May Be Your Own")

Onnie Jay Holy, Hoover Shoats, who "looked like an ex-preacher turned cowboy, or an ex-cowboy turned mortician." Had a radio program called "Soulsease, a quarter hour of Mood, Melody, and Mentality"; horns in on Hazel's "Church without Christ." (*WB*)

W. P. HOOTEN, Tanner's friend who worked at the railroad station in Corinth, Georgia. ("An Exile in the East" and "Judgement Day")

Joy-Hulga Hopewell, a thirty-two-year-old Ph.D. with an artificial leg and a weak heart; her belief in the philosophy of "nothing" leads her into a crippling situation. ("Good Country People")

Mrs. Hopewell, friend of Mrs. Freeman and Joy-Hulga's mother; talks in clichés, e.g., "nothing is perfect," and prides herself on her industry. ("Good Country People")

Mrs. Wallace Ben Hosen, neé Miss Hitchcock, another train passenger, on vacation from Chicago to Florida; name is changed in *WB* to Mrs. Wally Bee Hitchcock. ("The Train")

Annie Lou Jackson, train passenger who "had a hankering for people." ("The Train")

JACOBS, colleague of Rayber; "the philosophy man," who had a way of making "people think he knew more than Rayber thought he knew." ("The Barber")

Mr. Jerger, second floor, seventy-eight-year-old resident whom Ruby Hill thought peculiar; a former high school teacher, always trapping Ruby with "history questions that nobody knew." ("A Stroke of Good Fortune")

Joanne, Temple One, fourteen-year-old pupil at Mount St. Scholastica Convent; has nasal voice, yellow hair, and pimples. ("A Temple of the Holy Ghost")

Joe, the barber with whom Rayber argues about the Democratic White Primary Election. ("The Barber")

"John," an actor, the black neighbor of Tanner's sister. ("Judgement Day")

Rufus Johnson, age fourteen, I.Q. 140; previously in the reformatory, but adopted by Sheppard; father dead, mother in the pen, he was reared by his grandfather who beat him daily. He has a huge swollen foot and a "fanatic intelligence"; a thief at heart. ("The Lame Shall Enter First")

Julian, considers his mother dumpy, a bother, who depresses him. Tries to convince her that the new world is the real world and berates her. ("Everything That Rises Must Converge")

Julian's Mother, over fifty years old, between 165-200 pounds, with high blood pressure; speaks in banalities; takes pride in her ancestry; believes in separate-but-equal treatment of blacks, whom she patronizes. ("Everything That Rises Must Converge")

June Star, Bailey's daughter, a smart aleck, who tells Red Sam's wife that she "wouldn't live in a broken-down place like [Red Sam's Cafe] for a million bucks." ("A Good Man Is Hard to Find")

Miss Kirby, long-faced blond schoolteacher who boards at Susan and Joanne's house. ("A Temple of the Holy Ghost")

Lank-faced (Trashy) Woman, mother of dirty blond child and with the leathery old woman in the doctor's waiting room; wears a yellow sweat shirt, wine-colored slacks, and black-straw bedroom slippers with gold braid; dips snuff and labeled white trash by Mrs. Turpin. ("Revelation")

Solace Layfield, Hazel's "twin," who is a partner with Hoover Shoats and whom Haze runs down with his car. (*WB*)

Leathery Old Woman, in cotton print dress and tennis shoes; belongs with the lank-faced woman and blond child in the doctor's waiting room. ("Revelation")

Leola, Sheppard's cook, "a tall light-yellow girl with a mouth like a large rose" that had wilted. ("The Lame Shall Enter First")

LUCIA, does the dishes while Miss Willerton crumbs the table. ("The Crop")

LUTISHA, married to Rabie; a cook in Old Dudley's boarding house. ("The Geranium")

Mary Elizabeth, Calhoun's aunt's "sweet surprise" for him; but a kindred spirit to Calhoun about her feelings toward Partridge. ("The Partridge Festival")

Mary Grace, fat girl about eighteen years old, with acne, who sits in the doctor's waiting room reading and giving Mrs. Turpin spiteful looks; finally, she "attacks" Mrs. Turpin and calls her an "old wart hog." ("Revelation")

Mary Maud, Tilman's daughter, Walter's sister; a large woman of thirty years with childish face and carrot-colored hair; a schoolteacher. ("Why Do the Heathen Rage?")

MATTHEW, one of the young blacks who hunt the wildcat which Old Gabriel fears. ("Wildcat")

Aunt Mattie, Calhoun's other great-aunt: box-jawed, dead-white hair, and deaf. ("The Partridge Festival")

Maude, works as a waitress in the Frosty Bottle, the refreshment stand at City Forest Park, where Enoch Emery would stop; she knows a "clean boy" when she sees one. (*WB*)

Mrs. May, a small woman, near-sighted, with hair that "rose on top like the crest of some disturbed bird"; condescending toward the Greenleafs, but lacking conviction to fire Mr. Greenleaf. She has a respect for religion, but no belief in it. ("Greenleaf")

Scofield May, one of Mrs. May's sons, a "policy man," who sells insurance to blacks. ("Greenleaf")

Wesley May, the younger of Mrs. May's sons, with rheumatic fever at the age of seven; the more intellectual, a college teacher. ("Greenleaf")

HANE McFARNEY, Ruller's brother who had "gone bad." ("The Turkey")

Ruller McFarney, eleven-year-old who chases and catches the wounded turkey, which he shows off in town. ("The Turkey")

JUDGE McINTYRE, Mrs. McIntyre's first husband who died and was buried on the farm. "She had liked him" although she married him (twice her age) for his money; he died bankrupt. ("The Displaced Person")

MR. McINTYRE (?), Mrs. McIntyre's third husband whom she divorced because he was a drunk. ("The Displaced Person")

Mrs. McIntyre, a "small woman of sixty" with red bangs; she buried one husband, divorced two. Hires the Displaced Person to avoid bearing "the burdens" of her farm alone. ("The Displaced Person")

Meeks, copper flue salesman who professes the philosophy of "love" [for profit]. (*VBIA*)

Thin Minnie, another black who Old Gabriel believed "had a spell on her since when she was small" and therefore, was safe from the wildcat. ("Wildcat")

The Misfit, a graying escaped convict who wore silver-rimmed spectacles "that gave him a scholarly look," tight blue jeans, black hat, and no shirt. Believes "Jesus thrown everything off balance" and who says "no pleasure but meanness" in life. ("A Good Man Is Hard to Find")

Asa Moats, later Asa Hawks (q.v.) in *WB*. ("The Heart of the Park")

Sabbath Moats, Sabbath Lily Hawks (q.v.) in *WB*. ("The Heart of the Park")

MORGAN, light brown, part Indian—younger of two dairymen working for Mrs. Fox. ("The Enduring Chill")

Hazel Motes ("The Prophet"), age twenty-two, wears "glaring blue suit" with the price tag still stapled to the sleeve; eyes the color of pecan shells, nose like a shrike's bill. Starts "the church of truth without Jesus Christ Crucified," in which he is the only member; ultimately, he sees the light. (*WB*)

LOT MOTUN, object of Miss Willerton's fictional fantasy. ("The Crop")

Buford Munson, a "customer" at Old Tarwater's still, and the black who buries him. (*VBIA*)

Luella Munson, Buford's sister who helps Old Tarwater "kidnap" Rayber, Jr., the schoolteacher, when Rayber was seven years old. (*VBIA*)

ALONZO MYERS, eighteen-year-old, 250-pound driver hired to pick up the girls at the convent in Mayville. ("A Temple of the Holy Ghost")

WILLIE MYRICK, another one of the young blacks who hunts the wildcat which Old Gabriel fears. ("Wildcat")

Nancy, black who told of Hezuh's being killed by a wildcat. ("Wildcat")

Neighbor of Old Dudley's Daughter, calls Old Dudley, "old timer," and represents a different black than Old Dudley is willing to accept; wears pin-stripe suit, tan tie, shiny tan shoes. Helps Old Dudley up the stairs. ("The Geranium")

Nelson, Mr. Head's grandson, age ten, who is proud of being city-born until he visits the city with his grandfather. ("The Artificial Nigger")

Norton, Sheppard's son, a "stocky blond boy of ten" with large round ears, eyes slightly too far apart and one eye listing toward the outer rim; selfish. ("The Lame Shall Enter First")

OLD FELLOW, with a rusty hand spread out on each knee, pretends to sleep to avoid offering Mrs. Turpin a seat in the doctor's waiting room. ("Revelation")

OLD WOMAN, for whom Parker works; nearly seventy years old; about whom Parker concocts a fantasy to make his wife jealous. ("Parker's Back")

Mr. Paradise, the skeptic at the healing, who follows Bevel (Harry Ashfield) back to the River. He reminds Bevel of a giant pig. ("The River")

BETTY JEAN PARKER, Parker's mother who would not pay for his tattoos; a staunch Methodist. ("Parker's Back")

Obadiah Elihue Parker, a sullen person who seems to break everything he touches; receives a dishonorable discharge from the navy. His ultimate act is having "God" tattooed on his back. ("Parker's Back")

Sarah Ruth Parker, see Sarah Ruth Cates.

Parrum, train porter whom Hazel Motes accuses of being from Eastrod. (*WB*)

Coleman Parrum, an insolent drifter whom Tanner hired thirty years ago and whom Tanner describes as "stinking skin full of bones." ("Judgement Day")

Mr. Pitts, Mr. Fortune's son-in-law, father of seven children; "thin, long-jawed, irascible, sullen, sulking individual"; considered by Mr. Fortune to be an "idiot." ("A View of the Woods")

Mary Fortune Pitts, nine-year-old granddaughter who looks like her grandfather, Mr. Fortune; but who turns against him when he sells the Pitts's view of the woods. ("A View of the Woods")

Manley Pointer, backwoods' Bible salesman who dupes Hulga and makes the claim that Hulga "ain't so smart. [He's] been believing in nothing ever since [he] was born!" ("Good Country People")

George Poker, see General Sash.

PORTER, reminds Hazel of Old Cash, but denies the relationship; compare Parrum. ("The Train")

Potato-Peeler Salesman, tries to sell his gadgets from his "altar" on the temple of the streets; ignored by Hazel Motes. (*WB*).

Mrs. Pritchard, works on Mrs. Cope's farm, a large woman with a "shelf of stomach" and "a small pointed face and steady ferreting eyes"; she would go thirty miles to see someone laid away and always portrays a little voice of doom. ("A Circle in the Fire")

Rabie, Old Dudley's Wednesday fishing guide in Coa County and a handy-man at his boarding house; married to Lutisha. ("The Geranium")

RANDALL, older than Morgan, a "very black and fat" dairyman who works for Mrs. Fox. ("The Enduring Chill")

Rayber, the college teacher who tries to engage in a serious discourse at the barber shop and who is called a "Mother-Hubbard" because he sup-ports a "liberal" gubernatorial candidate. ("The Barber")

RAYBER'S WIFE, down-to-earth, not interested in his "higher" concerns. ("The Barber")

Bishop Rayber, dim-witted son of Bernice Bishop and Rayber; he was "like a child who had been a child for centuries." (*VBIA*)

George F. Rayber, Jr., Old Tarwater's nephew who wants to rear Francis Marion Tarwater; a schoolteacher by profession, he marries Bernice Bishop by whom they have one child, Bishop Rayber. Accepts the guilt of his fathers. (*VBIA*)

RAYBER, SR., married Old Tarwater's sister by whom he has a son, George F. Rayber, Jr.; an insurance salesman by trade. (*VBIA*)

Reba, the black who is superstitious about the cat and whose superstition is borne out. ("Wildcat")

Roosevelt, Tilman's yardman turned nurse. ("Why Do the Heathen Rage?")

Roy, "Fat Man," also, "the executive," who sides with Joe the barber re-garding political question of integration. ("The Barber")

RUFUS, Ruby's baby brother who is home from the army; age twenty. ("A Stroke of Good Fortune")

General Tennessee Flintrock Sash, George Poker, 104 years old; originally 5'4" of "pure game cock," but now frail as a dried spider, who sits on stage in his confederate uniform at his granddaughter's graduation from college. ("A Late Encounter with the Enemy")

John Wesley Poker Sash, Sally Poker's nephew, a Boy Scout expected to wheel General Sash on stage at Sally's graduation; fat, blond, age ten, with an executive expression. ("A Late Encounter with the Enemy")

Sally Poker Sash, General Sash's sixty-two-year-old granddaughter who, after twenty years of summer school, is graduating from college. She arranges to have her grandfather, in uniform, on the stage. ("A Late Encounter with the Enemy")

MRS. SCHMITT, Old Dudley's daughter's neighbor. ("The Geranium" and "An Exile in the East")

Sheppard, Norton's father and a widower; city recreational director and counselor at the reformatory where Rufus Johnson resides. Rejects his son to "save" Rufus. ("The Lame Shall Enter First")

Mr. Tom. T. Shiftlet, one-armed tramp, carpenter by trade, twenty-eight years old with a "look of composed dissatisfaction as if he understood life thoroughly"; marries Lucynell Crater's daughter. ("The Life You Save May Be Your Own")

Hoover Shoats, see Onnie Jay Holy.

ANNIE MAUDE SHORTLEY, going on fifteen and who "never got her growth." ("The Displaced Person")

Mr. Chancey Shortley, dairyman for Mrs. McIntyre; married to a woman whose instincts he follows; his "cigarette trick'" does "things" to Mrs. Shortley. ("The Displaced Person")

H. C. SHORTLEY, age twenty with a salesman's personality and who wants to become a preacher. ("The Displaced Person")

Mrs. Shortley, "Big Belly" to the blacks because of her mountainous stature: she "stood on two tremendous legs, with the grand self-confidence of a mountain"; a woman of visions. ("The Displaced Person")

SARAH MAE SHORTLEY, going on seventeen, the Shortley's daughter who has a cast in her eye. ("The Displaced Person")

Old Cash Simmons, see Porter.

Singleton, a "broad but bony and bleak face"; tried by a mock court for not buying an Azalea Festival Badge in Partridge; in retaliation, shoots six citizens; becomes the object of Calhoun's and Mary Elizabeth's quest. ("The Partridge Festival")

Slade, used car salesman who sells Hazel Motes the "high rat-colored machine with large thin wheels and bulging headlights." (WB)

SLADE'S BOY, wearing a black raincoat and a leather cap, he tries to hustle business for Slade. (WB)

Garfield Smith, one of three boys who bring destruction to Mrs. Cope's property; age thirteen, sullen, penetrating stare. ("A Circle in the Fire")

Stylish Lady, well-dressed—including red and gray suede shoes—gray-haired lady in the doctor's waiting room; has pleasant, sparkling blue eyes; the only person of whom Mrs. Turpin approves in that room. ("Revelation")

Sulk, works for Mrs. McIntyre, a "yellowish boy with a short woodchuck-like head"; whom Mr. Guizac wants to marry his cousin (in Poland) so she can come to the United States. ("The Displaced Person")

Reverend Bevel Summers, tall nineteen-year-old youth who as faith healer baptizes Harry Ashfield and who talks about the River of Life. ("The River")

Susan, Temple Two, a skinny, fourteen-year-old pupil at Mount St. Scholastica Convent; she has a pointed face, red hair; boy-crazy. ("A Temple of the Holy Ghost")

Franklyn R. T. Tanner, see T. C. Tanner. ("An Exile from the East")

T. C. Tanner, lives with his daughter in New York City and has shipping instructions pinned to his clothing in the event he is found dead. ("Judgement Day")

W. T. Tanner, see T. C. Tanner.

Tanner's Daughter, dawdles over everything; "holds" her father rather than allowing him to return to his own homeland. ("Judgement Day")

TANNER'S SON-IN-LAW, "stupid muscular face and yankee voice" who resents his father-in-law. ("Judgement Day")

Francis Marion Tarwater, "Frankie," fourteen year old who lives with his great-uncle, who said that he was a prophet; he fulfills his great uncle's prophecy and takes up the "message." (*VBIA*)

MASON TARWATER, Francis Marion's great-uncle, a self-proclaimed prophet, with silver protruding eyes, fierce in his attempts "to save" both Francis and Rayber. (*VBIA*)

Tattoo Artist, see Artist.

Temple One, see Joanne.

Temple Two, see Susan.

Thomas, a thirty-five-year-old historian who lives with his mother because of the comforts "home" provides: his books, home-cooked meals, an electric blanket; driven by an aggressive inner voice of his dead father, but Thomas lacks the ability to act. Shoots his mother accidentally. ("The Comforts of Home")

Thomas's Mother, a heavy body with an incongruous head; keeps a well-regulated house, serves excellent meals, and does the "nice thing to do"; invites Star Drake into their home. ("The Comforts of Home")

TILMAN, the owner of filling station/dance hall and sundry other businesses; he is the real threat to the Pitts's view of the woods. ("A View of the Woods")

Tilman, Walter's father; his left eye is twisted inward due to a stroke. ("Why Do the Heathen Rage?")

Tilman's Wife, who cannot understand her son, Walter, but who takes satisfaction in justice. ("Why Do the Heathen Rage?")

Claud Turpin, Mrs. Turpin's husband who is "florid, bald, sturdy"; an ulcer on his leg is the occasion for their being in the doctor's waiting room. ("Revelation")

Mrs. Ruby Turpin, a very large woman with bright black eyes, forty-seven years old; highly critical of the people in the doctor's waiting room and thankful that she is a "good woman"; Mary Grace attacks her. ("Revelation")

IGNATIUS VOGLE, S.J., the priest whom Asbury Fox meets at a lecture on Vedanta. ("The Enduring Chill")

Walter, Tilman's son; at age twenty-eight, a bland face, heavy jaw, non-committal lawyer's smile; who amuses himself writing letters to people he does not know. ("Why Do the Heathen Rage?")

Laverne Watts, special friend of Ruby, a tall, straw-haired girl of thirty years; secretary to a chiropodist; lives on third floor of Ruby's apartment building; interested in Rufus, Ruby's "baby" brother. ("A Stroke of Good Fortune")

Mrs. Leora Watts, prostitute whom Hazel Motes stays with his first night in Taulkinham; yellow hair, "white skin that glistened with greasy preparation," and a grin curved and as sharp as a sickle. (*WB*)

Miss Weatherman, see Mrs. Wally Bee Hitchcock.

Hazel Weaver, becomes Hazel Motes (q.v.) in *WB*. ("The Heart of the Park")

John Wesley, "a stocky child with glasses"; a smart-aleck; and a spoiled child. ("A Good Man Is Hard to Find")

Hazel Wickers, becomes Hazel Motes (q.v.) in *WB*; his mother, neé Jackson, from Eastrod, Tennessee. ("The Train")

Cory Wilkins, sixteen-year-old grandson of Mrs. Buchell and date for Temple One and Temple Two; thin, high cheek bones, pale seed-like eyes; sings hymns to the girls. ("A Temple of the Holy Ghost")

Wendell Wilkins, twin brother to Cory and other date for Temple One and Temple Two. ("A Temple of the Holy Ghost")

Miss Willerton, "Willie," forty-four-year-old writer who believes in "phonetic art," and who does not recognize a real story when she meets it on the street; internalizes her own characters. ("The Crop")

BOON WILLIAMS, one of the young blacks who hunt the wildcat that Old Gabriel fears. ("Wildcat")

Madam Zoleeda, palmist on Highway 87 who reads Ruby's future and predicts "a stroke of good fortune." ("A Stroke of Good Fortune")

5

O'Connor's Place in Twentieth-Century Literature

O'Connor's place in twentieth-century literature can be (and has been) assessed and is already secured in spite of the relatively small canon: twenty-five stories, two novels, fourteen essays, and a collection of letters. A religious writer who wrote religiously, O'Connor explains in a letter to Andrew Lytle, 15 September 1955, her "place" this way: "To my way of thinking, the only thing that keeps me from being a regional writer is being a Catholic and the only thing that keeps me from being a Catholic writer (in the narrow sense) is being a Southerner . . . " (*HB*, p. 104). To separate the two is an arbitrary delineation, made with the conviction "divide and conquer." Obviously the characteristics of each category are different, but the two fuse in O'Connor's work and neither draws inordinate attention to itself. For convenience, we shall be arbitrary in our approach, however.

O'CONNOR AS SOUTHERNER

Louis D. Rubin, Jr., provides a list of characteristics of Southern writers during the "Southern Renascence," a list which summarizes much of the earlier thought on this subject. These characteristics include:

a sense of the past, an uninhibited reliance upon the full resources of language and the old-fashioned moral absolutes that lay behind such language, an attitude toward evil as being present not only in economic or social forces but integral to the "fallen state" of humankind, a rich surface texture of description that would not be confined to the drab hues of the naturalistic novel, an ability to get at the full complexity of a situation rather than seeking to reduce it to its simplified essentials, a suspicion of abstractions, a bias in favor of the individual, the concrete, the unique, even the exaggerated and outlandish in human portraiture.[1]

Rubin's list describes the general southern writer in what Lewis P. Simpson has termed the "First Southern Renascence." In the "Second Southern Renascence," Simpson sees a shift of controlling conflict in the Southern literary imagination: "The struggle between the moral order of memory and history tends to be transformed into a struggle between gnostic[2] society and the existential self."[3] O'Connor belongs somewhere in between these last two.

At a Modern Language Association Special Session in San Francisco, 1979, John R. May raised the question of O'Connor's historical consciousness. Although history does not seem to dominate O'Connor's fiction, May pointed out that it is there in regional racial prejudice, in regional communication, in social class distinctions, and in the biblical, and therefore human, history of salvation. He concluded that "the stories in which the inner experience of the protagonists seems of greatest importance and is most successfully portrayed are those in O'Connor's canon with the broadest and most convincing social base, i.e., those in which a sense of historical community also dominates."[4] The stories which best exemplify her sense of historical community, I feel, are the stories about intellectuals, e.g., "Good Country People," "The Lame Shall Enter First," "The Barber," "A Late Encounter with the Enemy," and "The Enduring Chill." In them the intellectuals have received their formal educations and formed their ideas outside the community (the South) in which they were reared. Thus, we see or come to understand their community better when their ideas are juxtaposed to their parents' and to their communities' traditions. Hulga's supposed belief in Nothingness; Sheppard's sociological ideals to the exclusion of his son; Rayber's liberal political views in the barber shop; Sally Poker Sash's "historical" pride in "General" Sash, her grandfather; and Asbury's views of the artistic temper, respectively from the stories mentioned above. O'Connor seems to be saying, among other things that book learning in isolation of history, when taken in and of itself to the exclusion of everything else, leads to emptiness, calamity, personal degradation—to a personal blindness of one's own humanness and to a lack of direction.

In that sense, O'Connor as southerner is part of the historical consciousness with a deep sense of the past. She is in another way, too. In his essay "The Southern Novelist and Southern Nationalism," Lewis Simpson comments about Southern writers awakening to the South as a part of the apocalypse of modern civilization: "the revelation of the horror of a scientific-industrial-technological machine which operates completely on the principle of endless consumption, and is in fact consuming the world."[5] In O'Connor's fiction, Sheppard takes science (the telescope and microscope) as the means of "salvation" for Rufus; Hazel Motes's car becomes symbol of his escape from his past; the train is Mr. Head and Nelson's vehicle from and return to their own lives; and the bulldozer symbolizes progress for Mr. Fortune. The bulldozer is in fact consuming the land as Mr. Fortune sells parcels of land for development which will one day result in a complete town named, he hopes, in his honor. Again, O'Connor reveals a distrust in science and technology, in anything used to the exclusion of human understanding. Her mechanical imagery usually takes on a countenance which is menacing, or dilapidated, or destructive, to those who either do not take machines for what they are or who seek their answers solely through them.[6]

If it has been said correctly, as Robert Penn Warren suggests, "that the Southerner is incurably and incorrigibly historical-minded,"[7] then we might look for other Southern roots in O'Connor's writing as a way of defining her southernness. One such way is in the comic tradition. "Much of her work," writes Rubin, "appears rooted in the great comic tradition of Middle Georgia literature, which goes back to the old Southwestern humor of A. B. Longstreet and others in the early nineteenth century."[8] Longstreet was particularly good at describing places and portraying realistic characters, two of O'Connor's strong suits, and in identifying the foibles and eccentricities of local customs and manners which make people laughable.[9] Underlying it all, though, is a tension among characters, language, and action, a fine line which teeters on the brink of tragedy. Although O'Connor's stories often end in that tragedy—because the stakes are the highest, those of human souls—they are not without their humorous moments.

Exaggeration of characteristics and of incidents is one cause of our laughter in O'Connor's stories. Exaggeration brings to focus characters' peculiarities and dramatizes characters' mannerisms, even in their moment of difficulty. We, as readers, are relieved that it is happening in the story and not to us; we sense through the tension an impending doom and are glad for a momentary reprieve; and we are reminded, if the characters and scenes are realistically drawn, of a part of our lives. Thus, we are drawn to at least a wry smile as we share an experience in our humanness vicariously through the artist's creation. In O'Connor's work that technique also sets us up for the shock of the final action, but briefly we forget the seriousness at hand. For example, we can recognize the irony of Miss Willerton's living an exciting life in her romances while missing the excitement of life around her. We know what the fortune-teller means by a stroke of good fortune before Ruby is willing to admit to herself that she *is* pregnant. The grandmother in

"A Good Man Is Hard to Find" amuses us because she represents typically southern grandmothers, or as O'Connor writes to John Hawkes, 14 April 1960: "These old ladies exactly reflect the banalities of the society and the effect is of the comical rather than the seriously evil" (*HB*, p. 389). The image of John Wesley Poker Sash in his Boy Scout uniform wheeling General Sash at breakneck speed around the campus in "A Late Encounter with the Enemy" strikes our funny bone because his action is incongruous with the situation but not untypical of a ten-year-old boy. Julian's mother's hat is ludicrous; that she sees an exact duplicate get on the bus—after her vain preening in front of the mirror—is funny. Tanner's dream about his being shipped back home in a coffin and his springing out of it shouting "Judgement Day!" to frighten Coleman is based on an old practical joke. Yet, we laugh at it.

O'Connor's humor fits in the southern tradition and is comical because of her setting and the characters who inhabit it. It is not, nonetheless, limited to Southerners, but it does enhance her readers' appreciation of her country. As Eudora Welty writes in her essay "Place in Fiction," "one place comprehended can make us understand other places better. Sense of place gives equilibrium; extended, it is sense of direction too."[10] If we follow it to its intended end, O'Connor's direction leads us inevitably toward religion.

O'CONNOR AS CATHOLIC

As a religious writer, O'Connor swims against the tide of modern letters.[11] That reason alone, perhaps, makes her fiction difficult for modern readers to grasp. Coupled with the trend away from religious views, away from the "mystery of the Word," is Allen Tate's observation that a complete view of religion "predicts both success and failure."[12] O'Connor's view is complete in the sense that, for her, religion has a beginning, middle, and end and also in the sense that she has a basis for her convictions; her fiction reveals both success and failure in a religious sense. But she grapples with that mystery as she examines southern Protestantism and depicts hypocrisy and intolerance where she finds them.[13] Her fiction thus characterizes her by her vision[14] and that vision draws heavily from her Catholic faith.

From Catholicism comes O'Connor's sacramental vision. From the Council of Trent in 1545 the sacraments "were defined as real means of grace operated by Christ himself when the conditions he laid down are fulfilled."[15] Thus, through the sacraments, "the saving grace of our Lord's Incarnation and Atonement are conveyed to the members of the Church. . . . The gift of grace which God gives to us in baptism is called Regeneration . . . and the requirements for this gift of God are repentance and faith."[16] Both "The River" and *The Violent Bear It Away* deal directly with this sacrament. By exploring the sacraments and searching for the truth in her fiction, O'Connor is, according to her duty as a Catholic, reflecting "the objective realities, instead of the distorted caricatures of the truth which spring from ignorance, prejudice, and misunderstanding."[17] That Tarwater baptizes Bishop for the wrong reasons is of no consequence to the act itself. According to Saint Augustine: "Baptism does not depend on the merits of those by whom it is administered, but in its own sanctity and truth, *on account of Him by whom it has been instituted.*"[18]

When we as readers understand that "three elements are necessary to constitute a sacrament: (1) an outward sign, (2) instituted by Christ, (3) to give grace,"[19] we are better equipped to participate in and to appreciate O'Connor's fiction. Often that outward sign is in nature since, to O'Connor, grace and nature are inseparable. Mrs. Turpin is a case in point in "Revelation." Her "revelation" is precipitated by a severe blow to the head by, ironically, Mary Grace in the doctor's waiting room. Her moment arrives as she is hosing down seven shoats in their pig parlor. Like Job she accosts God: "What do you send me a message like that for? . . . Why me?" (*CS*, pp. 506-7). The light of sunset deepens and her surroundings take on a mysterious hue as she asks the final question: "Who do you think you are?" In her moment of defiance she has a vision that "the first will be last and the last first." Her moment past, she continues to stare at the trees in disbelief. Much has gone on in that climactic scene to summarize O'Connor's Catholicity, but mainly those three elements: the violence as outward sign, Christ in nature, and Mrs. Turpin's opportunity for repentance. In this story, it is failure rather than success of proffered Grace, I believe, that O'Connor predicts.

After saying all that, careful readers might note that O'Connor's concerns with death, grace, and the devil; her sacramental vision; and her concentration on the mysteries imbued in the realities of life are, as Sister Kathleen Feeley has observed, pertaining to Christian theology rather than to Catholic dogma.[20] O'Connor is a Catholic novelist much in the way Gerard Manley Hopkins is a Catholic poet. For them, "the beauty and worth of all things must be seen in and through the love of God."[21] That approach need not be ascribed to one denomination, to one faith: Bible-thumping Protestantism was all around her, but the mysteries remained the same regardless. The realities were just a little more dramatic to observe in her world.

O'CONNOR AS WOMAN WRITER

This section serves as postscript to the categories in which critics have placed O'Connor. As postscript it is not meant to diminish her contributions as a major woman writer of the twentieth century; the category itself does that. Why should writers, male and female, be separated and then evaluated? It is as if they cannot compete in the same arena, an absurd notion at the very least. What we may marvel at, however, is the literary imagination stemming from a person who appears (and is) unassuming, self-effacing, and overly shy. Her fiction is tougher than that of most of her counterparts, male and female. Indeed, the initial reaction to the name "Flannery O'Connor" is usually, "Who's *he*?" Nonetheless, the category has been established; and curricula thrive on course offerings featuring women in literature and literature by women. After such categories have been labeled, where do they go from there? Recognition is one thing; study, quite another. In the former, female characters, regardless of their author's gender, are fit subjects; and in the latter, female authors become the criterion, regardless of their characters' gender. To ignore one sex for the other becomes, in my opinion, simply wrong-headed in approach. O'Connor saw it that way, too.

Her characters are for the most part evenly divided between men and women. If women dominate her short fiction, men do so in her two novellas. Women characters are most often alone in her fiction, divorced, widowed, or simply single: Mrs. McIntyre has gone through three husbands, Hulga has never married. Her women characters have difficulties created in part by their society's beliefs about women, e.g., that they are less capable of running a farm—although O'Connor's women have run their respective places several years since their husbands' deaths—they are the homemakers; they are more easily duped (Mrs. May in "Greenleaf"). Stereotypes, but with an added dimension usually: their encounter with Grace.

Patricia Meyer Spacks suggests that "conceivably the relative invisibility of women writers reflects special critical difficulty in dealing with them."[22] O'Connor, though, is an exception to Spacks's observation. Critical difficulties have arisen because of subject matter and O'Connor's vision, not because of her gender. She continues to receive critical attention because of the substance of her fiction, because there is something there worth returning to. O'Connor eschews the popular subject of sex in most of her fiction, but she relies on violence with a difference: motivation. The characters who in her stories perpetrate violent acts are those characters whom she shows to be without God, to be avoiding contact with Him. Hazel Motes comes immediately to mind as he founds his Church Without Christ; Tarwater's uncle Rayber in *The Violent Bear It Away* is another.

The question whether a man could have written these stories is a moot point. Can one individual duplicate another? Not yet, at least. That individual variety gives us the smorgasbord of life, gives us more than thirteen ways to look at something. Consequently, I give this category short shrift and prefer to look at O'Connor's fiction in relation to the human condition rather than to the female condition. Her artistry deserves that consideration; her subject demands it.

Catholic and Christian Existentialist Influences

This appendix neither attempts nor pretends to be a complete accounting of either topic, Catholicism or Christian existentialism. It is a very brief introduction to some names of Catholics and existentialists whose works were known to O'Connor and whose ideas gave her cause to reflect on her own theological concerns. Those reflections seem to have resulted in a strengthening of her own convictions through support, or opposition, or both. The arrangement is alphabetical and selective.

BUBER, MARTIN (1878-1965), Austrian existential philosopher and Jewish theologian who played an active part in the Zionist movement. His religious studies led him to Chasidism (pious or godly), which involves devotion to traditional Hebrew Law and scribal interpretation and which is also the title of Jewish mystics. He was an active mystic supporting "sanctification of the daily life."[1] WORKS: *I and Thou* (1923), the relationship between man and things, the "I-It" relationship; *The Eclipse of God* (1932), about which O'Connor comments that it is very far from Catholic theology in the belief that man cannot participate in the Divine Life (*HB*, pp. 303-4).

GUARDINI, MSGR. ROMANO (1885-1968), German priest and theologian admired by O'Connor because she felt that he lacked the smugness which plagues American clergy in print. She also admired his book *The Lord*, about which she writes, "There is nothing like it anywhere, certainly not in this country" (*HB*, p. 304) and finds that "the human condition includes both states [affirmative and negative] in truth and 'art' " (*HB*, p. 173). WORKS: *The Lord, The Conversion of St. Augustine, The Church and Modern Man*, and *The End of the Modern World*.

HEIDEGGER, MARTIN (1889-1976), German philosopher whose "main aim is to construct an ontology on the basis of which it will be possible to understand both the achievements and the failures of the history of Western metaphysics."[2] Some ideas which prevail in O'Connor's stories: (1) "Death is the end whereby a man's existence becomes complete . . . , that unique potentiality of *Dasein* [being-there]."[3] (2) For Heidegger, what underlies a participation in essential truth is "mystery," a mystery which "pervades" the whole of human existence.[4] (3) "The fundamental way in which we become attuned to the Nothingness attending what-is is anxiety,"[5] which seems to be Hulga's problem in "Good Country People." WORKS: *Being and Time* (1929), *Introduction to Metaphysics* (1935), *Letter on Humanism* (1949).

JASPERS, KARL (1883-1969), German psychologist and philosopher who stressed the limits of science, "notably its inability to reach the self" (*ODCC*, p. 716). If O'Connor did not know his writings, she nevertheless shared some of his ideas. About Jaspers' conviction about truth, David E. Roberts writes: "What makes the Exception valuable is not his unconventionality; the deviant may be a criminal instead of a prophet. . . . The distinguishing mark of the Exception is that he finds himself subject to an unconditional claim which is not objectively demonstrable."[6] For example, the Misfit in "A Good Man Is Hard to Find." And Jaspers' belief that "the task of actually participating in what we talk about becomes endless, and faith in Christ offers not a *substitute* for living out our lives but a call to self-realization"[7] appears in *Wise Blood* and *The Violent Bear It Away*. One of his essential themes is man's infinite capacity limited by himself: "Man is always more than what he knows, or can know, about himself."[8] WORKS: *Psychology of World Conceptions* (1919), *Man in the Modern Age* (1931), *Philosophy* (3 vols., 1932), *Philosophical Faith* (1948).

KIERKEGAARD, SØREN (1813-1855), Danish philosopher reared in the Danish State Lutheran Church. His "Concept of Dread" examines the whole complex of sin and redemption; his religious works show a "profound understanding of the redemptive work of Christ and the meaning of the Cross" (*ODCC*, p. 766). He sees modern man ignoring fate; when "man attempts to be the Absolute, human life can be pathetic or comic, but never tragic." Loss of the tragic is related to loss of the religious dimension in Kierkegaard,[9] and in O'Connor, as well. WORKS: Either/Or (1843), representing a choice between the aesthetic and ethical attitudes toward life; *The Concept of Dread* (1844); *Christian Discourses* (1850); *Training in Christianity* (1849-50).

MARCEL, M. GABRIEL (1889-1973), French existential philosopher who moved from agnosticism to Roman Catholicism. O'Connor viewed Marcel with mixed emotions, enjoying the Gifford Lectures (*Mystery of Being*), but "not making head or tail of" *The Philosophy of Existence*. Marcel writes that "the only genuine inward mutation is . . . inconceivable without . . . grace"[10]; and he deals with the distinction between problem and mystery: problem—"everything which occurs is 'purely natural' " and mystery—involvement in what is being sought to understand, e.g., love, evil[11] as in "The Lame Shall Enter First." Too, there is a grateful awareness "that God reveals Himself as generosity" which leads to apprehension of all life and one's own life as gifts of grace.[12] Marcel sees that "human life may become a temple which enshrines a gracious Presence,"[13] as in "A Temple of the Holy Ghost." WORKS: *The Philosophy of Existence* (ca. 1945), *The Mystery of Being* (1951), *Man Against Mass Society* (1951), *Being and Having* (1957).

MARITAIN, JACQUES (1882-1973), French Thomist philosopher. According to Sally Fitzgerald's introduction to *The Habit of Being*, it was in Maritain's *Art and Scholasticism* that O'Connor first learned the idea of "habit of art" (p. xvii). From him, she also developed some of her "literary theories": "Art is a virtue of the practical mind" (*MM*, pp. 64-65), and ". . . art is wholly concerned with the good of that which is made; it has no utilitarian end. If you do manage to use it successfully for special, religious, or other purposes, it is because you make it art first . . ." (*HB*, p. 157). Maritain recognized the dependence of human knowledge on sense experience and the need for reason and grace in a religious life (*ODCC*, p. 858). WORKS: *Art and Scholasticism with Other Essays* (1920), applies Thomist principles to aesthetics; *The Degrees of Knowledge* (1932); *Moral Philosophy* (1960).

MAURIAC, FRANÇOIS (1885-1970), French Catholic novelist whose religious crisis in 1928 led to his major themes of faith, sin, and divine grace. He is one of the Catholic writers who O'Connor says has influence (*HB*, p. 130). He attempts to make "the Catholic Universe of evil palpable, tangible, odorous."[14] WORKS: *Questions of Precedence* (1952?), *Destinies* (1928), *God and Mammon* (trans., 1936), *The Stumbling Block* (trans., 1952).

MERTON, THOMAS (1915-1968), French theologian, philosopher, and poet who entered the Trappist monastery of Gethsemani in 1941 and was ordained into the priesthood in 1949. WORKS: *The Seven Storey Mountain* (1948), autobiographical; *Seeds of Contemplation* (1949); *Waters of Siloe* (1949); *No Man Is an Island* (1955); *Spiritual Direction and Meditation* (1960).

PASCAL, BLAISE (1623-1662), French theologian and mathematician who was converted to Jansenism in 1654. He believed "(1) that without a special grace from God, the performance of His commandments is impossible to men, and (2) that the operation of grace is irresistible . . ." (*ODCC*, p. 714). His religion centered on the Person of Christ as Saviour, and he stressed "the polarity between faith and reason in a way that came quite close to Protestantism."[15] From his following beliefs, we are reminded of Tarwater in *The Violent Bear It Away*: (1) "Man, of his own nature, has always the power of sinning and of resisting grace," but (2) Pascal sees no conflict between human freedom and divine grace. (3) "In his misery and greatness, man is a contradiction, a mystery, a torment to himself."[16] Pascal's contradiction of man—greatness and wretchedness—is what O'Connor uses to best effect in her fiction: the "good" which is not all good, the "bad" which is not all bad. For Pascal, there are three orders of knowing: senses, reason, and faith. And he observes, ". . . the main obstacle to faith is not honest self-doubt but arrogant self-will,"[17] from which many of O'Connor's characters suffer. WORKS: *Provincial Letters* (1655); *Thoughts* (1670-unfinished), a vindication of the truth of Christianity.

SARTRE, JEAN-PAUL (1905-1980), French existential philosopher and writer. His philosophy attempts to overcome four great dichotomies in Western thought: mind vs. matter, reality vs. appearance, determinism vs. free will, and rationalism vs. irrationalism; and he distinguished between the thing as it is in itself and in human consciousness.[18] Alienation, Sartre says, is a basic characteristic of man's relationships. If so, we can better understand Rufus in "The Lame Shall Enter First." Sartre rejects belief in God as "irreconcilable with belief in human freedom"[19]; hence, man creates his own values, as do many of O'Connor's characters such as Shiftlet in "The Life You Save May Be Your Own." Roberts sees Sartre's service for theologians "by protesting against any doctrine of divine grace which does less than justice to freedom" (p. 255). His final word is that life remains absurd, a point which O'Connor uses to advantage when her characters are not receptive to Christ. WORKS: *Being and Nothingness* (1943), *Dirty Hands* (play, 1948), *Critique of Dialectical Reason* (1960).

SAINT AUGUSTINE (354-430), a Manichaean and Neo-Platonist before he was baptized into Christianity in 387. His importance is his understanding of Christian truth, specifically that God was sole creator of all things (against Manichaeanistic beliefs), the Church was "one" through the mutual charity of its members and "holy" because her purposes are holy, and man's salvation is through the grace of God (*ODCC*, p. 107). O'Connor quotes Saint Augustine both in her letters and her essays, and she views the senses as having divine origins, a belief set forth in his writings. WORKS: *Confessions* (ca. 400), *City of God* (413-426).

SAINT IGNATIUS LOYOLA (1491?-1556), founder of the Jesuits around 1540. His three endeavors were reformation of the Church from within, spreading the Gospel throughout the world, and fighting heresy. O'Connor refers to his statement, "the end sanctifies the means" (*HB*, p. 362); and the priest's name in "The Enduring Chill" is Ignatius Vogle, S.J. WORK: *Spiritual Exercises* (1522-1523), written during his self-purgation in Manresa shortly after his conversion.

SAINT THOMAS AQUINAS (1225-1274), Dominican philosopher and theologian, and Aristotelian in his theory of knowledge from sense perception, that is, from the natural world. His *Summa* is the accepted basis of modern Roman Catholic theology. Fundamental is his distinction between reason and faith: Christian truths lie beyond but are not contrary to reason; they reach us through revelation. Acceptance (faith) is a moral decision. Also, the sacraments are instituted by Christ with the eucharist the highest among the seven (*ODCC*, pp. 1352-53). O'Connor reports that she used to read the *Summa* every night before going to sleep (*HB*, p. 94). She repeatedly states that she is a Thomist through and through, a point she confirms in her essays and stories. For example, "According to St. Thomas, prophetic vision is not a matter of seeing clearly, but of seeing what is distant, hidden" (*HB*, p. 365). Tarwater cannot see what is hidden, but does accept prophetic vision on faith in *The Violent Bear It Away*. WORKS: *Summa Theologica* (1265-1271?), *Quaestiones Disputatae de Veritate* (1256-1259), *Catena Aurea* (ca. 1263).

TEILHARD DE CHARDIN, MARIE JOSEPH PIERRE (1881-1955), French theologian and paleontologist who helped discover the Peking Man. From him, O'Connor learned the phrase "passive diminishment," that is, serene acceptance of what must be (*HB*, p. 509). In one of his physical propositions she found the title for her collection of stories, *Everything That Rises Must Converge* (*HB*, p. 438). Teilhard believed that the Church fulfills a continuing evolutionary purpose; and his writings place man at the center of the cosmos and situates Christianity in human history as man in nature. WORKS:

The Phenomenon of Man (1959), *The Divine Milieu* (1960), *Letters from a Traveler* (1962), *Man's Place in Nature* (1966).

VOEGELIN, ERIC (1901-), German historian who believed in man's total participation in being, "the whole of his existence." O'Connor comments that Voegelin sees history "as an exodus from civilization" (*HB*, p. 294). WORKS: *The New Science of Politics* (1952), *Order and History* (4 vols., 1956-1974), *Science, Politics, and Gnosticism* (1968).

VON HÜGEL, BARON FRIEDRICH (1852-1925), Roman Catholic theologian and philosopher, founder of the London Society for the Study of Religion in 1905. He was concerned with the relation of Christianity to history, the place of human culture in the Christian life, the Christian conception of time, and the significance of eschatology in the modern world (*ODCC*, p. 1429). O'Connor finds "the Baron's spirit is an antidote to much of the vulgarity and rawness of American Catholics" (*HB*, p. 331). About materialism, she observes "that [his] most used words are derivatives of the word *cost*" (*HB*, p. 336). Her story, "A View of the Woods," projects away from materialism, a symbol of society's turning away from God. WORKS: *The Mystical Element of Religion* (1908), *Eternal Life* (1912), *Essays and Addresses on the Philosophy of Religion* (1921), *Letters to a Niece* (1928).

"Introduction to *A Memoir of Mary Ann*" by Flannery O'Connor

Stories of pious children tend to be false. This may be because they are told by adults, who see virtue where their subjects would see only a practical course of action; or it may be because such stories are written to edify and what is written to edify usually ends by amusing. For my part, I have never cared to read about little boys who build altars and play they are priests, or about little girls who dress up as nuns, or about those pious Protestant children who lack this equipment but brighten the corners where they are.

In the spring of 1960 I received a letter from Sister Evangelist, the Sister Superior of Our Lady of Perpetual Help Free Cancer Home in Atlanta. "This is a strange request," the letter read, "but we will try to tell our story as briefly as possible. In 1949, a little three-year-old girl, Mary Ann, was admitted to our Home as a patient. She proved to be a remarkable child and lived until she was twelve. Of those nine years, much is to be told. Patients, visitors, Sisters, all were influenced in some way by this afflicted child. Yet one never thought of her as afflicted. True she had been born with a tumor on the side of her face; one eye had been removed, but the other eye sparkled, twinkled, danced mischievously, and after one meeting one never was conscious of her physical defect but recognized only the beautiful brave spirit and felt the joy of such contact. Now Mary Ann's story should be written but who to write it?"

Not me, I said to myself.

"We have had offers from nuns and others but we don't want a pious little recital. We want a story with a real impact on other lives just as Mary Ann herself had that impact on each life she touched. . . . This wouldn't have to be a factual story. It could be a novel with many other characters but the outstanding character, Mary Ann."

A novel, I thought. Horrors.

Sister Evangelist ended by inviting me to write Mary Ann's story and to come up and spend a few days at the Home in Atlanta and "imbibe the atmosphere" where the little girl had lived for nine years.

It is always difficult to get across to people who are not professional writers that a talent to write does not mean a talent to write anything at all. I did not wish to imbibe Mary Ann's atmosphere. I was not capable of writing her story. Sister Evangelist had enclosed a picture of the child. I had glanced at it when I first opened the letter, and had put it quickly aside. Now I picked it up to give it a last cursory look before returning it to the Sisters. It showed a little girl in her First Communion dress and veil. She was sitting on a bench, holding something I could not make out. Her small face was straight and bright on one side. The other side was protuberant, the eye was bandaged, the nose and mouth crowded slightly out of place. The child looked out at her observer with an obvious happiness and composure. I continued to gaze at the picture long after I had thought to be finished with it.

After a while I got up and went to the bookcase and took out a volume of Nathaniel Hawthorne's stories. The Dominican Congregation to which the nuns belong who had taken care of Mary Ann had been founded by Hawthorne's daughter, Rose. The child's picture had brought to mind his story, "The Birthmark." I found the story and opened it at that wonderful section of dialogue where Alymer first mentions his wife's defect to her.

One day Alymer say gazing at his wife with a trouble in his countenance that grew stronger until he spoke.

"Georgiana," said he, "has it never occurred to you that the mark upon your cheek might be removed?"

"No, indeed," said she, smiling; but perceiving the seriousness of his manner, she blushed deeply. "To tell you the truth it has been so often called a charm that I was simple enough to imagine that it might be so."

"Ah, upon another face perhaps it might," replied her husband, "but never on yours. No, dearest Georgiana, you came so nearly perfect from the hand of Nature that this slightest defect, which we hesitate whether to term a defect or a beauty, shocks me, as being the visible mark of earthly imperfection."

"Shocks you, my husband!" cried Georgiana, deeply hurt, at first reddening with momentary anger, but then bursting into tears. "Then why did you take me from my mother's side? You cannot love what shocks you!"

The defect on Mary Ann's cheek could not have been mistaken for a charm. It was plainly grotesque. She belonged to fact and not to fancy. I conceived it my duty to write Sister Evangelist that if anything were written about this child, it should indeed be a "factual story," and I went on to say that if anyone should write these facts, it should be the Sisters themselves, who had known and nursed her. I felt this strongly. At the same time I wanted to make it plain that I was not the one to write the factual story, and there is no quicker way to get out of a job than to prescribe it for those who have prescribed it for you. I added that should they decide to take my advice, I would be glad to help them with the preparation of their manuscript and do any small editing that proved necessary. I had no doubt that this was safe generosity. I did not expect to hear from them again.

In *Our Old Home*, Hawthorne tells about a fastidious gentleman who, while going through a Liverpool workhouse, was followed by a wretched and rheumy child, so awful-looking that he could not decide what sex it was. The child followed him about until it decided to put itself in front of him in a mute appeal to be held. The fastidious gentleman, after a pause that was significant for himself, picked it up and held it. Hawthorne comments upon this:

Nevertheless, it could be no easy thing for him to do, he being a person burdened with more than an Englishman's customary reserve, shy of actual contact with human beings, afflicted with a peculiar distaste for whatever was ugly, and, further-more, accustomed to that habit of observation from an insulated standpoint which is said (but I hope erroneously) to have the tendency of putting ice into the blood.

So I watched the struggle in his mind with a good deal of interest, and am seriously of the opinion that he did a heroic act and effected more than he dreamed of toward his final salvation when he took up the loathsome child and caressed it as tenderly as if he had been its father.

What Hawthorne neglected to add is that he was the gentleman who did this. His wife, after his death, published his notebooks in which there was this account of the incident:

After this, we went to the ward where the children were kept, and, on entering this, we saw, in the first place, two or three unlovely and unwholesome little imps, who were lazily playing together. One of them (a child about six years old, but I know not whether girl or boy) immediately took the strangest fancy for me. It was a wretched, pale, half-torpid little thing, with a humor in its eye which the Governor said was the scurvy. I never saw, till a few moments afterward, a child that I should feel less inclined to fondle. But this little sickly, humor-eaten fright prowled around me, taking hold of my skirts, following at my heels, and at last held up its hands, smiled in my face, and standing directly before me, insisted on my taking it up! Not that it said a word, for I rather think it was underwitted, and could not talk; but its face expressed such perfect confidence that it was going to be taken up and made much of, that it was impossible not to do it. It was as if God had promised the child this favor on my behalf, and that I must needs fulfill the contract. I held my undesirable burden a little while, and after setting the child down, it still followed me, holding two of my fingers and playing with them, just as if it were a child of my own. It was a foundling, and out of all human kind it chose me to be its father! We went upstairs into another ward; and on coming down again there was this same child waiting for me, with a sickly smile around its defaced mouth, and in its dim-red eyes . . . I should never have forgiven myself if I had repelled its advances.

Rose Hawthorne, Mother Alphonsa in religious life, later wrote that the account of this incident in the Liverpool workhouse seemed to her to contain the greatest words her father ever wrote.

The work of Hawthorne's daughter is perhaps known by few in this country where it should be known by all. She discovered much that he sought, and fulfilled in a practical way the hidden desires of his life. The ice in the blood which he feared, and which this very fear preserved him from, was turned by her into a warmth which initiated action. If he observed, fearfully but truthfully; if he acted, reluctantly but firmly, she charged ahead, secure in the path his truthfulness had outlined for her.

Toward the end of the nineteenth century, she became aware of the plight of the cancerous poor in New York and was stricken by it. Charity patients with incurable cancer were not kept in the city hospitals but were sent to Blackwell's Island or left to find their own place to die. In either case, it was a matter of being left to rot. Rose Hawthorne Lathrop was a woman of great force and energy. A few years earlier she had become a Catholic and had since been seeking the kind of occupation that would be a practical fulfillment of her conversion. With almost no money of her own, she moved into a tenement in the worst section of New York and began to take in incurable cancer patients. She was joined later by a young portrait painter, Alice Huber, whose steady and patient qualities complemented her own forceful and exuberant ones. With their concerted effort, the grueling work prospered. Eventually other women came to help them, and they became a congregation of nuns in the Dominican Order—the Servants of Relief for Incurable Cancer. There are now seven of their free cancer homes over the country.

Mother Alphonsa inherited a fair share of her father's literary gift. Her account of the grandson of her first patient makes fine reading. He was a lad who, for reasons unpreventable, had been brought to live for a while in the tenement apartment with his ailing grandmother and the few other patients there at the time.

The boy was brought by an officer of the institution, to remain for a visit. My first glance at his rosy, healthy, clever face struck a warning shiver through my soul. He was a flourishing slip from criminal roots. His eyes had the sturdy gaze of satanic vigor . . . I began to teach him the catechism. With the utmost good nature he sat in front of me as long as I would sit, giving correct answers. "He likes to study it better than to be idle," said his grandmother; "and I taught it to him myself, long ago." His eyes took on a mystic vagueness during these lessons, and I felt certain he would tell the truth in future and be gentle instead of barbaric.

Food was hidden away in dark corners for the cherubic, overfed pet, and his pranks and thefts were shielded and denied, and the nice clothing I provided him with, out of our stores, with a new suit for Sundays, strangely disappeared when Willie went to call upon his mother. . . . In a few weeks Willie had become famous in the neighborhood as the worst boy it had ever experienced, although it was lined with little scoundrels. The inmates of the house and adjacent shanties feared him, the scoundrels made circles around him as he flew from one escapade to another on the diabolical street which was never free from some sort of outrages perpetrated by young or old. Willie built fires upon the shed roofs, threw bricks that guardian angels alone averted from our heads, and actually hit several little boys at sundry times, whom we mended in the Relief Room. He uttered exclamations that hideously rang in the ears of the profane themselves. . . . He delighted in the pictures of the saints which I gave him, stole those I did not give, and sold them all. I preached affectionately, and he listened tenderly, and promised to "remember," and was very sorry for his sins when he had been forced by an iron grasp to accept their revelation. He made a very favorble impression upon an experienced priest who was summoned to rescue his soul; and he built a particularly large bonfire on our woodshed when let go. The poor grandmother began to have severe hemorrhages, because of the shocks she received and the scoldings she gave. Before he came she used to call him "that little angel." Now she wisely declared that he was good-hearted.

Bad children are harder to endure than good ones, but they are easier to read about, and I congratulated myself on having minimized the possibility of a book about Mary Ann by suggesting that the Sisters do it themselves. Although I heard from Sister Evangelist that they were about it, I felt that a few attempts to capture Mary Ann in writing would lead them to think better of the project. It was doubtful that any of them had the literary gifts of their foundress. Moreover, they were busy nurses and had their hands full following a strenuous vocation.

Their manuscript arrived the first of August. After I had gathered myself together, I sat down and began to read it. There was everything about the writing to make the professional writer groan. Most of it was reported, very little rendered; at the dramatic moment—where there was one—the observer seemed to fade away, and where an exact word or phrase was needed, a vague one was usually supplied. Yet when I had finished reading, I remained for some time, the imperfections of the writing forgotten, thinking about the mystery of Mary Ann. They had managed to convey it.

The story was as unfinished as the child's face. Both seemed to have been left, like creation on the seventh day, to be finished by others. The reader would have to make something of the story as Mary Ann had made something of her face.

She and the Sisters who had taught her had fashioned from her unfinished face the material of her death. The creative action of the Christian's life is to prepare his death in Christ. It is a continuous action in which this world's goods are utilized to the fullest, both positive gifts and what Père Teilhard de Chardin calls "passive diminishments." Mary Ann's diminishment was extreme, but she was equipped by natural intelligence and by a suitable education, not simply to endure it, but to build upon it. She was an extraordinarily rich little girl.

Death is the theme of much modern literature. There is *Death in Venice, Death of a Salesman, Death in the Afternoon, Death of a Man*. Mary Ann's was the death of a child. It was simpler than any of these, yet infinitely more knowing. When she entered the door of Our Lady of Perpetual Help Home in Atlanta, she fell into the hands of women who were shocked at nothing and who love life so much that they spend their own lives making comfortable those who have been pronounced incurable of cancer. Her own prognosis was six months, but she lived twelve years, long enough for the Sisters to teach her what alone could have been of importance to her. Hers was an education for death, but not one carried on obtrusively. Her days were full of dogs and party dresses, of Sisters and sisters, of Coca-Colas and Dagwood sandwiches, and of her many and varied friends—from Mr. Slack and Mr. Connolly to Lucius, the yard man; from patients afflicted the way she was to children who were brought to the Home to visit her and were perhaps told when they left to think how thankful they should be that God had made their faces straight. It is doubtful if any of them were as fortunate as Mary Ann.

The Sisters had set all this down artlessly and had devoted a good deal of their space to detailing Mary Ann's many pious deeds. I was tempted to edit away a good many of these. They had willingly given me the right to cut, and I could have laid about me with satisfaction but for the fact that there was nothing with which to fill in any gaps I created. I felt too that while their style had been affected by traditional hagiography and even a little by Parson Weems, what they had set down was what had happened and there was no way to get around it. This was a child brought up by seventeen nuns; she was what she was, and the itchy hand of the fiction writer would have to be stayed. I was only capable of dealing with another Willie.

I later suggested to Sister Evangelist, on an occasion when some of the Sisters came down to spend the afternoon with me to discuss the manuscript, that Mary Ann could not have been much *but* good, considering her environment. Sister Evangelist leaned over the arm of her chair and give me a look. Her eyes were blue and unpredictable behind spectacles that unmoored them slightly. "We've had some demons!" she said, and a gesture of her hand dismissed my ignorance.

After an afternoon with them, I decided that they had had about everything and flinched before nothing, even though one of them asked me during the course of the visit why I wrote about such grotesque characters, why the grotesque (of all things) was my vocation. They had in the meantime inspected some of my writing. I was struggling to get off the hook she had me on when another of our guests supplied the one answer that would make it immediately plain to all of them. "It's your vocation too," he said to her.

This opened up for me also a new perspective on the grotesque. Most of us have learned to be dispassionate about evil, to look it in the face and find, as often as not, our own grinning reflections with which we do not argue, but good is another matter. Few have stared at that long enough to accept the fact that its face too is grotesque, that in us the good is something under construction. The modes of evil usually receive worthy expression. The modes of good have to be satisfied with a cliché or a smoothing-down that will soften their real look. When we look into the face of good, we are liable to see a face like Mary Ann's, full of promise.

Bishop Hyland preached Mary Ann's funeral sermon. He said that the world would ask why Mary Ann should die. He was thinking undoubtedly of those who had known her and knew that she loved life, knew that her grip on a hamburger had once been so strong that she had fallen through the back of a chair without dropping it, or that some months before her death, she and Sister Loretta had got a real baby to nurse. The Bishop was speaking to her family and friends. He could not have been thinking of that world, much farther removed yet everywhere, which would not ask why Mary Ann should die, but why she should be born in the first place.

One of the tendencies of our age is to use the suffering of children to discredit the goodness of God, and once you have discredited His goodness, you are done with Him. The Alymers whom Hawthorne saw as a menace have multiplied. Busy cutting down human imperfection, they are making headway also on the raw material of good. Ivan Karamazov cannot believe, as long as one child is in torment; Camus' hero cannot accept the divinity of Christ, because of the massacre of the innocents. In this popular pity, we mark our gain in sensibility and our loss in vision. If other ages felt less, they saw more, even though they saw with the blind, prophetical, unsentimental eye of acceptance, which is to say, of faith. In the absence of this faith now, we govern by tenderness. It is a tenderness which, long since cut off from the person of Christ, is wrapped in theory. When tenderness is detached from the source of tenderness, its logical outcome is terror. It ends in forced-labor camps and in the fumes of the gas chamber.

These reflections seem a long way from the simplicity and innocence of Mary Ann; but they are not so far removed. Hawthorne could have put them in a fable and shown us what to fear. In the end, I cannot think of Mary Ann without thinking also of that fastidious, skeptical New Englander who feared the ice in his blood. There is a direct line between the incident in the Liverpool workhouse, the work of Hawthorne's daughter, and Mary Ann—who stands not only for herself but for all the other examples of human imperfection and grotesquerie which the Sisters of Rose Hawthorne's order spend their lives caring for. Their work is the tree sprung from Hawthorne's small act of Christlikeness and Mary Ann is its flower. By reason of the fear, the search, and the charity that marked his life and influenced his daughter's, Mary Ann inherited, a century later, the wealth of Catholic wisdom that taught her what to make of her death. Hawthorne gave what he did not have himself.

This action by which charity grows invisibly among us, entwining the living and the dead, is called by the Church the Communion of Saints. It is a communion created upon human imperfection, created from what we make of our grotesque state. Of hers Mary Ann made what, like all good things, would have escaped notice had not the Sisters and many others been affected by it and wished it written down. The Sisters who composed the memoir have told me that they feel they have failed to create her as she was, that she was more lively than they managed to make her, more gay, more gracious, but I think that they have done enough and done it well. I think that for the reader this story will illuminate the lines that join the most diverse lives and that hold us fast in Christ.

Notes

PREFACE

1. Robert Penn Warren, "Why Do We Read Fiction?" in Cleanth Brooks, John Thibaut Purser, and Robert Penn Warren, *An Approach to Literature*, alt. 4th ed. (New York: Appleton-Century-Crofts, 1967), pp. 866-72.

2. John Gardner, *On Moral Fiction* (New York: Basic Books, Inc., 1978), p.120.

1: INTRODUCTION: ON READING
FLANNERY O'CONNOR

1. The article "Sign of the Wolf," *Time*, 25 July 1977, p. 58, discusses lupus in lay terms.

2. *The Complete Stories* (New York: Farrar, Straus and Giroux, 1971), p. 133. Subsequent quotations from O'Connor's works will be abbreviated and cited parenthetically within the text. *See* Abbreviations and Selected Bibliography.

3. Because of the relevance of this particular topic in O'Connor's fiction, readers might also see Arthur Koestler, *Dialogue with Death*, trans. Trevor and Phyllis Blewitt (New York: Macmillan Company, 1946).

4. *Robert Penn Warren Talking: Interviews 1950-1978*, ed. Floyd C. Watkins and John T. Hiers (New York: Random House, 1980), p. 129.

5. Thomas Swiss, "The Principle of Apprenticeship: Donald Justice's Poetry," *Modern Poetry Studies*, 10 (1980), 44.

6. John Gardner, *On Moral Fiction* (New York: Basic Books, Inc., 1978), pp. 110 ff. Gardner makes this point explicitly in his section entitled "Moral Fiction."

7. In her essay "The Teaching of Literature," O'Connor states that "the mystery

of existence is always showing through the texture of their [poor people's] ordinary lives . . ." (*MM*, p. 133). Chapter 2 of this book discusses O'Connor's essays, which provide clear statements about her theories on literature. That collection and her edited letters are significant companions to her fiction.

8. Quoted in Gardner, p. 106.

9. Gardner, p. 83.

10. Gardner, p. 120.

11. Martin Heidegger, *Existence and Being*, trans. R. F. C. Hull and Alan Crick (Chicago: Henry Regnery Company, 1949), p. 359.

12. See Thomas Merton, "The Other Side of Despair: Notes on Christian Existentialism," *Critic*, 24 (October-November 1965), 12-23.

13. O'Connor comments specifically on this scene in *The Habit of Being*, ed. Sally Fitzgerald (New York: Farrar, Straus and Giroux, 1979), p. 275.

14. Huston Smith, *The Religions of Man* (New York: New American Library, 1959), p. 302.

15. Smith, p. 311.

16. Laura [Riding] Jackson narrows the consideration: "The problem of good and evil is not the problem of good and evil, but only the problem of evil. . . ." *The Telling* (New York: Harper & Row, 1972), p. 140.

17. For one group of outsiders' views on a southern community, see Roger Williams, "The Yankee Transplant," *Signature*, June 1977, pp. 29-32, 64, about the Grumman Corporation's move from Long Island to Milledgeville.

18. Cleanth Brooks, in *The Relationship of the Alabama-Georgia Dialect to the Provincial Dialects of Great Britain* (Baton Rouge: Louisiana State University Press, 1935), has analyzed those speech patterns closely.

19. Alfred M. Kern, author of *The Width of Waters, Made in U.S.A.*, and *The Trial of Martin Ross*, and Visiting Professor of English, United States Air Force Academy, 1979-80, gave me that definition of manners on 31 October 1979.

20. About one facet of southern manners, Daniel J. Boorstin writes, "The Southern gentleman's Code of Honor—for all the minutiae of his duelling handbook—had to be learned at his mother's knee; it could be known only to the initiate." *The National Experience*, vol. II of *The Americans* (New York: Vintage Books, 1965), p. 211.

21. Robert Penn Warren, *All the King's Men* (New York: Harcourt, Brace and Company, 1946), pp. 462, 463.

22. Lewis P. Simpson, "The Southern Novelist and Southern Nationalism," in *The Man of Letters in New England and the South* (Baton Rouge: Louisiana State University Press, 1973), p. 202.

2: THE NONFICTION

1. E. M. Forster, *Aspects of the Novel* (New York: Harcourt, Brace & World, Inc., 1954), p. 3. Recipes for gazpacho, a cold vegetable soup, vary slightly, but the basic ingredients include ripe tomatoes, cucumbers, bell peppers, onions, and seasonings, a mixture which when properly blended provides a pleasing taste.

2. Robert Fitzgerald, "Introduction," in Flannery O'Connor, *Everything That Rises Must Converge* (New York: Farrar, Straus, and Giroux, 1965), p. xxxii.

3. Cleanth Brooks and Robert Penn Warren, *Understanding Fiction* (New York: Appleton-Century-Crofts, Inc., 1943), p. 605. O'Connor refers to her use of *Understanding Fiction* numerous times in her letters.

4. Laura [Riding] Jackson, *The Telling* (New York: Harper & Row, 1972), p. 70.

5. Fitzgerald, p. xxvii.

6. Wayne C. Booth, *The Rhetoric of Fiction* (Chicago: University of Chicago Press, 1961), p. 74.

7. Dorothy Walters, *Flannery O'Connor* (New York: Twayne Publishers, Inc., 1973), p. 14.

8. In this study, I am including "An Exile in the East" and "Judgement Day" with the example of "The Geranium" since they are simply different versions of the same story.

9. Although O'Connor does not mention her source, "what-is" comes from the German existential philosopher, Martin Heidegger, in his essay "On the Essence of Truth."

10. O'Connor alludes to Manichaeanism in "The Fiction Writer and His Country" (*MM*, p. 33), "The Nature and Aim of Fiction" (*MM*, p. 68), and "The Church and the Fiction Writer" (*MM*, p. 147).

3: THE FICTION

1. O'Connor explains this effect in a letter to a Professor of English (*HB*, p. 437).

2. Thomas Merton, "The Other Side of Despair: Notes on Christian Existentialism," *Critic*, 24 (October-November 1965), 17.

3. By the "supernatural" I am suggesting something that man can perceive but not explain, as in religious "mystery." Contrarily, "natural" implies something that man can perceive and can explain through empirical evidence or scientific law.

4. The person who picks Tarwater up and subsequently rapes him wears a lavender shirt, a thin black suit, and a panama hat (*VBIA*, p. 227).

5. Howard C. Brashers, *Creative Writing* (New York: American Book Company, 1968), p. 24.

6. Excerpts from finished novels, though they are included in *The Complete Stories*, are not discussed as short fiction, i.e., "The Train," "The Peeler," "The Heart of the Park," and "Enoch and the Gorilla" from *WB* and "You Can't Be Any Poorer Than Dead" from *VBIA*.

7. Robert Giroux, "Introduction," in *The Complete Stories*, by Flannery O'Connor (New York: Farrar, Straus and Giroux, 1971), p. xvi.

8. Marcel Proust, *Swann's Way*, trans. C. K. Scott Moncrieff (New York: Random House, 1934), p. 36. The tea and taste of madeleines become an associative device which jogs the narrator's memory.

9. From the word "geranium," *ger* is "echoic of a hoarse cry," similar perhaps to the one Old Dudley makes when his throat tightens up, an occurrence each time he is confronted with his sense of loss of place.

10. Jan Nordby Gretlund, "Flannery O'Connor's 'An Exile in the East': An Introduction," *South Carolina Review*, 11 (1978), 4.

11. Gretlund, p. 11.

12. I find Gregor Sebba's comment telling: "For the Gnostic, the world is a strange place into which man is 'thrown,' not knowing why nor how. It is a labyrinth through which alienated man errs, seeking to come home without knowing the way." "Orders and Disorders of the Soul: Eric Voegelin's Philosophy of History," *Southern Review*, NS 3 (Spring 1967), 302.

13. Ralph C. Wood, "From Fashionable Tolerance to Unfashionable Redemption: A Reading of Flannery O'Connor's First and Last Stories," *Flannery O'Connor Bulletin*, 7 (1978), 23.

14. Sebba, p. 301.

15. *Cleanth Brooks at the United States Air Force Academy*, ed. James A. Grimshaw, Jr. (USAFA: Department of English, 1980), p. 41.

16. The choice of the name Lot is one of O'Connor's ways of having fun in her stories. The Biblical name means "veil" and certainly in the story Miss Willerton's world is obscured from reality. Too, it is Lot's wife who during their escape from Sodom looks back and is turned into a pillar of salt (Genesis 19:26).

17. In the story, "Willie" (1. 5) is also spelled "Willy" (1. 19; *CS*, p. 38). Among four manuscripts of this story, the "y" seems to have been the favored spelling. The difference is of little consequence, it seems to me, except to note that Willy and Willie are one and the same character.

18. Sister Kathleen Feeley, S.S.N.D., *Flannery O'Connor: Voice of the Peacock* (New Brunswick, NJ: Rutgers University Press, 1972), p. 128.

19. According to Mr. Gerald Becham, Curator of the O'Connor Collection at Georgia College, Ruby was originally Haze Motes's sister in *Wise Blood*, which in the expanded version provided more background on Haze. See *HB*, p. 101.

20. Reminiscent of Shakespeare's lines: "Nothing in his life / Became him like the leaving it" (*Macbeth*, I.iv.7-8).

21. Sister Feeley references a passage marked by O'Connor in Martin Buber's *The Eclipse of God* (p. 36) which pertains theologically to the Misfit's psychological being: his "fear of God," p. 75.

22. According to Mary Barbara Tate, Atkinson Auditorium at Georgia College is the setting for this story, a setting O'Connor would have known from her own college days there.

23. The image of vampires is associative and serves as another manifestation of evil. I am not suggesting any literal parallel and do not mean to imply that O'Connor here drifts into the occult.

24. For *CS*, "The Displaced Person" shows three labeled divisions; I have merely subdivided them further.

25. David Eggenschwiler, *The Christian Humanism of Flannery O'Connor* (Detroit, MI: Wayne State University Press, 1972), p. 95.

26. *Stephen Crane: Stories and Tales*, ed. Robert Wooster Stallman (New York: Vintage Books, 1958), pp. 316-17.

27. *Tantum ergo*: ["Down in adoration falling . . ."], by Saint Thomas Aquinas. Trans. E. Caswall (1849), *Maryknoll Missal* (New York: P. J. Kenedy & Sons,

1966), hymn #13. A hymn sung during the benediction. I am indebted to Mrs. Audrey Gatlin for this reference.

28. Marion Montgomery deals with this phrase from Saint Paul in "Flannery O'Connor, Eric Voegelin, and the Question That Lies Between Them," *Modern Age*, 22 (1978), 137.

29. Nathaniel Hawthorne explores this idea in "My Kinsman, Major Molineux," in terms not unfamiliar to O'Connor, who considred him "a very great writer indeed" (*HB*, p. 70).

30. F. L. Cross, ed., *The Oxford Dictionary of the Christian Church* (London: Oxford University Press, 1957), p. 846.

31. O'Connor's point in a letter to "A," 24 August 1956 (*HB*, p. 171).

32. John R. May, *The Pruning Word: The Parables of Flannery O'Connor* (Notre Dame: University of Notre Dame Press, 1976), p. 100.

33. O'Connor, *HB*, p. 190.

34. Vedānta: "The fundamental thought of Advaita Vedānta is that the life-monad or embodied soul (*jīva*) is in essence the self (*ātman*), which being beyond the changing, transient, phenomenal apparitions of our empirical experience, is none other than Brahman, the sole and universal Eternal Reality, which is beyond change, self-effulgent and ever free, and defined as 'one-without-a-second' (*a-dritīya*), 'really existing' (*sat*), 'purely spiritual' (*cit*) and 'sher bliss' (*ānandae*)." Heinrich Zimmer, *Philosophies of India*, ed. Joseph Campbell (Cleveland: World Publishing Company, 1956), p. 456.

35. The image of the Spirit descending like a dove is mentioned in Mark 1:10.

36. O'Connor takes the title from Pierre Teilhard de Chardin's writing (*HB*, p. 438).

37. Douglas Rhymes, *Forward Day by Day*, May-July 1977, p. 70. Based on the 8 July reading from Matthew 18:21-35.

38. Feeley, p. 105.

39. An idea introduced early in the story (*CS*, p. 423) and suggesting the Jungian concept of the "undiscovered self" as Sister Feeley and others have pointed out.

40. *Cleanth Brooks at the United States Air Force Academy*, p. 43.

41. Joseph Campbell examines science versus religion in a provocative essay, "The Impact of Science on Myth" in *Myths to Live By* (New York: Bantam Books, 1973), pp. 1-18.

42. Ed Nelson, "Flannery O'Connor: A Religious Experience," *Columns* (Georgia College), Fall 1975, pp. 6-8.

43. In an 8 Nov 63 letter to Cecil Dawkins, O'Connor suggests that she was planning to include "The Enduring Chill" as a section in the new novel (*HB*, p. 546).

44. Cf. Luke 18:11: "The Pharisee stood and prayed thus with himself, God, I thank thee, that I am not as other men *are*, extortioners, unjust, adulterers, or even as this publican."

45. For the distinctions among "short novel," "nouvelle," "novella," and "novelette," all as intermediate lengths between the short story and novel, see C. Hugh Holman, *A Handbook to Literature*, 4th ed. (Indianapolis: Odyssey Press, 1979).

46. *Wise Blood* (New York: Farrar, Straus and Giroux, 1962), p. [5]; rpt. in *Mystery and Manners*, pp. 114-15.

47. For a fuller account of the meaning of Haze's name, see James A. Grimshaw, Jr., *"Le Mot Juste:* Hazel Motes's Name," *Notes on Modern American Literature,* 3 (Spring 1979), item 14.

48. For an interpretation of the title, see John R. May, *"The Violent Bear It Away:* The Meaning of the Title," *Flannery O'Connor Bulletin,* 2 (1973), 83-86.

49. Eudora Welty, "Some Notes on Time in Fiction," *Mississippi Quarterly,* 26 (Fall 1973), 490; quoted in Lewis P. Simpson, "The Southern Aesthetic of Memory," *Tulane Studies in English,* 23 (1978), 214-15.

50. From Brainard Cheney's letters, Special Collections, Vanderbilt University Library, Nashville, Tennessee.

51. This novella is O'Connor's most complex genealogical work. We have three generations with which to deal:

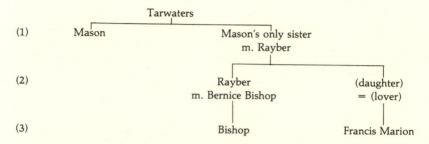

52. *HB,* pp. 359-60; O'Connor mentions that she was reading about some cases of possession in the nineteenth century and beliefs about the Devil's capacity for deception—which relates indirectly to *VBIA.*

53. This interpretation is surely open to some discussion since, literally, unction is administered to the sick, to the dangerously ill. But according to the Council of Trent, its chief effects "are the conferring of grace, the remission of sins, and the alleviation of the sick" (O'Brien, p. 274).

4: A KALEIDOSCOPE OF CHARACTERS

1. Regarding this name, see James A. Grimshaw, Jr., "The Mistaken Identity of Rufus [Florida] Johnson," *Notes on Modern American Literature,* 1 (Fall 1977), item 31.

5: O'CONNOR'S PLACE IN TWENTIETH-CENTURY LITERATURE

1. Louis D. Rubin, Jr., *The Literary South* (New York: John Wiley & Sons, 1979), pp. 411-12.

2. Gnostic = supporting intuitive knowledge in spiritual matters. For more on this belief, see Eric Voegelin, *Israel and Revelation,* Vol. I of *Order and History* (Baton Rouge: Louisiana State University Press, 1956), and his *Science, Politics, and Gnosticism* (Chicago: Henry Regnery, 1968).

3. Lewis P. Simpson, *The Dispossessed Garden: Pastoral and History in Southern Literature*, Mercer University Lamar Memorial Lectures, No. 16 (Athens: University of Georgia Press, 1975), p. 90.

4. John R. May, "Stalking Joy: Flannery O'Connor and the Habit of Living Within" (p. 5), in William H. Slavick, moderator, "The Question of the Southern Renascence and the Inner Experience: Porter, Gordon, Agee, O'Connor, and Percy," MLA Special Session No. 641, 30 December 1979. Mimeographed copies of the papers were available at the session.

5. Lewis Simpson, *The Man of Letters in New England and the South: Essays on the History of the Literary Vocation in America* (Baton Rouge: Louisiana State University Press, 1973), p. 226.

6. In his book *The Machine in the Garden: Technology and the Pastoral Ideal in America* (New York: Oxford University Press, 1964), Leo Marx examines more closely the effects of mechanization on literary imaginations, especially those in the nineteenth century but equally applicable to those in the twentieth century.

7. Robert Penn Warren, "Introduction" to *A Southern Harvest* (Boston: Houghton Mifflin Co., 1937), p. xiv.

8. Rubin, p. 689,

9. Henning Cohen and William B. Dillingham, eds., *Humor of the Old Southwest* (Boston: Houghton Mifflin Co., 1964). Their introduction provides a good brief sketch of the elements of humor in the early southwest tales.

10. Eudora Welty, *The Eye of the Story: Selected Essays and Reviews* (New York: Random House, 1978), pp. 128-29.

11. Lewis P. Simpson notes in his essay, "The Southern Writer and the Great Literary Secession," that the "whole modern effect toward the renewal of letters, . . . ultimately is an expression of an increasing alienation of modern man from the mystery of the Word" in *The Man of Letters in New England and the South*, p. 254.

12. Allen Tate, "Religion and the Old South," in *Essays of Four Decades* (New York: William Morrow & Co., Inc., 1963), p. 561.

13. Rubin, p. 416.

14. This is as she says it should be in *Mystery and Manners*, p. 179.

15. Bonnell Spencer, O.H.C., *Ye Are the Body: A People's History of the Church*, rev. ed. (West Park, NY: Holy Cross Publications, 1965), p. 229.

16. Rev. Jerome F. Politzer, "A Form of Godliness," *The Anglican Digest*, Autumn 1979, p. 5.

17. Rev. John A. O'Brien, *The Faith of Millions: The Credentials of the Catholic Religion*, rev. ed. (Huntington, IN: Our Sunday Visitor, 1938), p. 57.

18. Quoted in O'Brien, p. 165.

19. O'Brien, p. 161.

20. *Flannery O'Connor: Voice of the Peacock* (New Brunswick, NJ: Rutgers University Press, 1972), pp. 6, et passim.

21. W. H. Gardner, ed., *Poems of Gerard Manley Hopkins*, 3rd ed. (New York: Oxford University Press, 1948), p. xxv.

22. Patricia Meyer Spacks, "Introduction," in *Contemporary Women Novelists: A Collection of Critical Essays*, Twentieth-Century Views (Englewood Cliffs, NJ:

Prentice-Hall, Inc., 1977), p. 1. Surely Ms. Spacks jests, though, or the statement could be taken as a "put down" to women writers everywhere.

APPENDIX 1: CATHOLIC AND CHRISTIAN EXISTENTIALIST INFLUENCES

1. F. L. Cross, ed., *The Oxford Dictionary of the Christian Church* (London: Oxford University Press, 1957), p. 204. Subsequent quotations from this reference are cited parenthetically with the abbreviation *ODCC*.

2. David E. Roberts, *Existentialism and Religious Belief*, ed. Roger Hazelton (New York: Oxford University Press, 1959), p. 147. Because of its breadth and clarity, I have referred frequently to this edition.

3. Roberts, p. 154.

4. Roberts, p. 169.

5. Roberts, p. 176.

6. Roberts, p. 257.

7. Roberts, p. 271.

8. Daniel O'Connor, "Jaspers," in *The McGraw-Hill Encyclopedia of World Biography*, Vol. 5 (New York: McGraw-Hill Book Co., 1973), p. 537.

9. Roberts, p. 66.

10. Roberts, p. 280.

11. Roberts, p. 283.

12. Roberts, p. 318.

13. Roberts, p. 331.

14. Denis Boak in *The McGraw-Hill Encyclopedia of World Biography*, pp. 7, 264.

15. Roberts, p. 15.

16. Roberts, pp. 30, 33, and 41, respectively.

17. Roberts, pp. 50, 52.

18. Roberts, pp. 197, 198.

19. Roberts, p. 216.

Selected Bibliography

This checklist is neither exhaustive nor perfunctory; it is selective. What it does do, therefore, is offer some titles of critical works by categories. The categories, in turn, suggest some approaches to O'Connor's works: biographical, genre, general, comparative, topical. Even among the approaches, I have made selections; not all the authors with whom O'Connor can be compared, for example, are listed. The amount of attention and the variety of approaches to O'Connor's works increase yearly. Existing bibliographies—*Modern Language Association Bibliography* and *Modern Humanities Research Association Annual Bibliography*—continue their yearly coverage of recent publications and should surely be consulted also. This checklist provides readers with a utilitarian list of titles by and about O'Connor; and it should serve as a convenient starting point.

Within each heading and subheading, except the first, entries are arranged alphabetically by authors' last name. The first category, a list of O'Connor's books, is arranged chronologically. Various editions of her works, her personal library, the manuscripts, much of her correspondence, and extensive holdings of critical studies about her writing are housed in the Flannery O'Connor Collection, Georgia College, Milledgeville, Georgia. The *Flannery O'Connor Bulletin* (hereafter cited as *FOB*), an annual publication, is also published at Georgia College.

O'CONNOR'S WORKS

Wise Blood. New York: Harcourt, Brace, 1952.
A Good Man Is Hard to Find. New York: Harcourt, Brace, 1955.

The Violent Bear It Away. New York: Farrar, Straus and Cudahy, 1960.

Everything That Rises Must Converge. New York: Farrar, Straus and Giroux, 1965.

Mystery and Manners: Occasional Prose. Edited by Sally and Robert Fitzgerald. New York: Farrar, Straus and Giroux, 1969.

Flannery O'Connor: The Complete Stories. New York: Farrar, Straus and Giroux, 1971.

Flannery O'Connor: The Habit of Being. Letters edited by Sally Fitzgerald. New York: Farrar, Straus and Giroux, 1979.

CHECKLISTS

Becham, Gerald. "The Flannery O'Connor Collection." *FOB*, 1 (1972), 66-71.

Brittain, Joan T. "Flannery O'Connor: A Bibliography, Part I." *Bulletin of Bibliography*, 25 (September-December 1967), 98-100; "Part II." 25 (January-April 1968), 123-24; "Addenda." 25 (May-August 1968), 142.

Dunn, Robert J. "The Manuscripts of Flannery O'Connor at Georgia College." *FOB*, 5 (1976), 61-69.

Friedman, Melvin J. "Flannery O'Connor." In *A Bibliographical Guide to the Study of Southern Literature.* Edited by Louis D. Rubin, Jr. Baton Rouge: Louisiana State University Press, 1969, pp. 250-53.

Golden, Robert E., and Mary C. Sullivan. *Flannery O'Connor and Caroline Gordon: A Reference Guide.* Boston: G. K. Hall, 1977.

Newman, Georgia Ann. "Flannery O'Connor: An Annotated Bibliography of Secondary Sources, 1952-1969." M.A. Thesis, Florida State University, 1969.

Williams, Jerry T., comp. *Southern Literature, 1968-1975: A Checklist of Scholarship.* Boston: G. K. Hall, 1978, pp. 168-75.

Wray, Virginia F. "Flannery O'Connor." In *First Printings of American Authors.* Edited by Matthew J. Bruccoli and C. E. Frazer Clark. Detroit: Gale Research Company, 1977. I, 281-83.

BIOGRAPHICAL INFORMATION

Coles, Robert. "Flannery O'Connor: A Southern Intellectual." *Southern Review*, NS 16 (1980), 46-64.

_____. "Flannery O'Connor: Letters Larger than Life." *FOB*, 8 (1979), 3-13.

Drake, Robert. *Flannery O'Connor: A Critical Essay.* Contemporary Writers in Christian Perspective Series. Grand Rapids: William B. Eerdmans, 1966.

Fitzgerald, Robert. "Introduction." In *Everything That Rises Must Converge.* New York: Farrar, Straus and Giroux, 1965, pp. vii-xxxiv.

Hicks, Granville. "A Writer at Home with Her Heritage." *Saturday Review*, 12 May 1962, pp. 22-23.

Hoy, Cyrus, and Walter Sullivan, eds. "An Interview with Flannry O'Connor and Robert Penn Warren." *Vagabond* (Vanderbilt University), 6 (February 1960), 9-17; rpt. in *Robert Penn Warren Talking: Interviews 1950-1978.* Edited by Floyd C. Watkins and John T. Hiers. New York: Random House, 1980, pp. 54-69.

Kirk, Russell. "Memoir by Humpty-Dumpty." *FOB*, 8 (1979), 14-17.

Lee, Maryat. "Flannery, 1957." *FOB*, 5 (1976), 39-60.

McKenzie, Barbara. "Flannery O'Connor Country on Film: A Photo Essay." *Georgia Review*, 31 (1977), 404-26.

Mullins, C. Ross, Jr. "Flannery O'Connor: An Interview." *Jubilee*, June 1963, pp. 33-35.

Tate, James. "An O'Connor Remembrance." Unpublished typescript, March 1967, 6 pp.

Walston, Rose Lee. "Flannery: An Affectionate Recollection." *FOB*, 1 (1972), 55-60.

Williams, Roger. "The Yankee Transplant." *Signature*, June 1977, pp. 29-32, 64.

CRITICAL ARTICLES ON THE NOVELS

THE VIOLENT BEAR IT AWAY

Brinkmeyer, Robert H., Jr. "Borne Away by Violence: The Reader and Flannery O'Connor." *Southern Review*, NS 15 (1979), 313-21.

Burns, Stuart L. "Flannery O'Connor's *The Violent Bear It Away*: Apotheosis in Failure." *Sewanee Review*, 76 (1968), 319-36.

Mayer, David R. "*The Violent Bear It Away*: Flannery O'Connor's Shaman." *Southern Literary Journal*, 4 (1972), 41-54.

McCowen, Robert M., S.J. "The Education of a Prophet: A Study of Flannery O'Connor's *The Violent Bear It Away*." *Kansas Magazine* (Kansas State University, Manhattan), 1962, pp. 73-78.

Muller, Gilbert. "*The Violent Bear It Away*: Moral and Dramatic Sense." *Renascence*, 22 (1969), 17-25.

Rosenfield, Claire. "The Shadow Within: The Conscious and Unconscious Use of the Double." *Daedalus*, 92 (1963), 326-44.

Smith, Francis J., S.J. "O'Connor's Religious Viewpoint in *The Violent Bear It Away*." *Renascence*, 22 (1970), 108-12.

Trowbridge, Clinton W. "The Symbolic Vision of Flannery O'Connor: Patterns of Imagery in *The Violent Bear It Away*." *Sewanee Review*, 76 (1968), 298-318.

Wray, Virginia F. "An Authorial Clue to the Significance of the Title *The Violent Bear It Away*." *FOB*, 6 (1977), 107-8.

WISE BLOOD

Asals, Frederick. "Flannery O'Connor as Novelist: A Defense." *FOB*, 3 (1974), 23-39.

———. "The Road to *Wise Blood*." *Renascence*, 21 (1969), 181-94.

Baumbach, Jonathan. *The Landscape of Nightmare: Studies in the Contemporary American Novel*. New York: New York University Press, 1965, pp. 87-100.

Chow, Sung Gay. " 'Strange and Alien Country': An Analysis of Landscape in Flannery O'Connor's *Wise Blood* and *The Violent Bear It Away*." *FOB*, 8 (1979), 35-44.

Dula, Martha A. "Evidences of the Prelapsarian in Flannery O'Connor's *Wise Blood*." *Xavier University Studies*, 11 (1972), 1-12.

Gordon, Caroline. "Flannery O'Connor's *Wise Blood*. *Critique*, 2 (1958), 3-10.

Graulich, Melody. " 'They Ain't Nothing But Words': Flannery O'Connor's *Wise Blood*." *FOB*, 7 (1978), 64-83.

Green, James L. "Enoch Emery and His Biblical Namesakes in *Wise Blood*." *Studies in Short Fiction*, 10 (1973), 417-19.

Gregory, Donald. "Enoch Emery: Ironic Doubling in *Wise Blood*." *FOB*, 4 (1975), 52-64.

Grimshaw, James A., Jr. "*Le Mot Juste*: Hazel Motes's Name." *Notes on Modern American Literature*, 3 (1979), item 14.

Harrison, Margaret. "Hazel Motes in Transit: A Comparison of Two Versions of Flannery O'Connor's 'The Train' with Chapter 1 of *Wise Blood*." *Studies in Short Fiction*, 8 (1971), 287-93.

Lawson, Lewis A. "Flannery O'Connor and the Grotesque: *Wise Blood*." *Renascence*, 17 (1965), 137-47.

LeClair, Thomas. "Flannery O'Connor's *Wise Blood*: The Oedipal Theme." *Mississippi Quarterly*, 29 (1976), 197-205.

Littlefield, Daniel F. "Flannery O'Connor's *Wise Blood*: 'Unparalleled Prosperity and Spiritual Chaos.'" *Mississippi Quarterly*, 23 (1970), 121-33.

Lorch, Thomas M. "Flannery O'Connor: Christian Allegorist." *Critique*, 10 (1968), 69-80.

McCullagh, James C. "Aspects of Jansenism in Flannery O'Connor's *Wise Blood*." *Studies in the Humanities*, 3 (1972), 12-16.

————. "Symbolism and the Religious Aesthetic: Flannery O'Connor's *Wise Blood*." *FOB*, 2 (1973), 43-58.

Rechnitz, Robert M. "Passionate Pilgrim: Flannery O'Connor's *Wise Blood*." *Georgia Review*, 19 (1965), 310-16.

CRITICAL ARTICLES ON THE STORIES

"THE ARTIFICIAL NIGGER"

Byrd, Turner F. "Ironic Dimension in Flannery O'Connor's 'The Artificial Nigger.'" *Mississippi Quarterly*, 21 (1968), 243-51.

Hays, Peter L. "Dante, Tobit, and 'The Artificial Nigger.'" *Studies in Short Fiction*, 5 (1968), 263-68.

Kahane, Claire. "Artificial Nigger." *Massachusetts Review*, 19 (1978), 183-98.

Rubin, Louis D., Jr. "Flannery O'Connor's Company of Southerners: Or, 'The Artificial Nigger' Read as Fiction Rather Than Theology." *FOB*, 6 (1977), 47-71.

"THE COMFORTS OF HOME"

Millichap, Joseph R. "The Pauline 'Old Man' in Flannery O'Connor's 'The Comforts of Home.'" *Studies in Short Fiction*, 11 (1974), 96-99.

"THE DISPLACED PERSON"

Fitzgerald, Robert. "The Countryside and the True Country." *Sewanee Review*, 70 (1962), 380-94.

Joselyn, Sister M., O.S.B. "Thematic Centers in 'The Displaced Person.'" *Studies in Short Fiction*, 1 (1964), 85-92.

Male, Roy R. "The Two Versions of 'The Displaced Person.'" *Studies in Short Fiction*, 7 (1970), 450-57.

"EVERYTHING THAT RISES MUST CONVERGE"

Denham, Robert. "The World of Guilt and Sorrow: Flannery O'Connor's 'Everything That Rises Must Converge.'" *FOB*, 4 (1975), 42-51.

Desmond, John F. "The Lessons of History: Flannery O'Connor's 'Everything That Rises Must Converge.'" *FOB*, 1 (1972), 39-45.

Fowler, Doreen Ferlaino. "Mrs. Chestney's Saving Graces." *FOB*, 6 (1977), 99-106.

Hopkins, Mary Frances. "Julian's Mother." *FOB*, 7 (1978), 114-15.

Maida, Patricia D. "'Convergence' in Flannery O'Connor's 'Everything That Rises Must Converge.'" *Studies in Short Fiction*, 7 (1970), 549-55.

Montgomery, Marion. "On Flannery O'Connor's 'Everything That Rises Must Converge.'" *Critique: Studies in Modern Fiction*, 13 (1971), 15-29.

Oates, Joyce Carol. "The Visionary Art of Flannery O'Connor." *Southern Humanities Review*, 7 (1973), 235-46.

Rubin, Louis D., Jr. "Southerners and Jews." *Southern Review*, NS 2 (1966), 697-713.

"AN EXILE IN THE EAST"

Gretlund, Jan N. "Flannery O'Connor's 'An Exile in the East': An Introduction." *South Carolina Review*, 11 (1978), 3-11.

"THE GERANIUM"

Wood, Ralph C. "From Fashionable Tolerance to Unfashionable Redemption: A Reading of Flannery O'Connor's First and Last Stories." *FOB*, 7 (1978), 10-25.

"GOOD COUNTRY PEOPLE"

Pierce, Constance. "The Mechanical World of 'Good Country People.'" *FOB*, 5 (1976), 30-38.

Smith, Anneliese H. "O'Connor's 'Good Country People.'" *Explicator*, 33 (1974), item 30.

"A GOOD MAN IS HARD TO FIND"

Bellamy, Michael O. "Everything Off Balance: Protestant Election in Flannery O'Connor's 'A Good Man Is Hard to Find.'" *FOB*, 8 (1979), 116-24.

Brittain, Joan T. "O'Connor's *A Good Man Is Hard to Find*."*Explicator*, 26 (1967), item 1.

Ellis, James. "Watermelons and Coca-Cola in 'A Good Man Is Hard to Find': Holy Communion in the South." *Notes on Contemporary Literature*, 8, no. 3 (1978), 7-8.

Kropf, C. R. "Theme and Setting in 'A Good Man Is Hard to Find.'" *Renascence*, 24 (1972), 177-80, 206.

Marks, W. S., III. "Advertisements for Grace: Flannery O'Connor's 'A Good Man Is Hard to Find.'" *Studies in Short Fiction*, 4 (1966), 19-27.

Martin, Sister M., O.P. "O'Connor's 'A Good Man Is Hard to Find.'" *Explicator*, 24 (1965), item 19.

Merton, Thomas "The Other Side of Despair: Notes on Christian Existentialism." *Critic*, 24 (October-November 1965), 12-23.

Montgomery, Marion. "Miss Flannery's 'Good Man.'" *Denver Quarterly*, 3 (1968), 1-17.

Portch, Stephen R. "O'Connor's 'A Good Man Is Hard to Find.'" *Explicator*, 37, no. 1 (1978), 19-20.

Quinn, John J., S.J. "A Reading of Flannery O'Connor." *Thought*, 48 (1973), 520-31.

Rubin, Louis D., Jr. "Two Ladies of the South." *Sewanee Review*, 63 (1955), 671-81.

Woodward, Robert H. "A Good Route Is Hard to Find: Place Names and Setting in O'Connor's 'A Good Man Is Hard to Find.'" *Notes on Contemporary Literature*, 3 (1973), 2-6.

"GREENLEAF"

Asals, Frederick. "The Mythic Dimensions of Flannery O'Connor's 'Greenleaf.'" *Studies in Short Fiction*, 5 (1968), 317-30.

"THE LAME SHALL ENTER FIRST"

Asals, Frederick. "Flannery O'Connor's 'The Lame Shall Enter First.'" *Mississippi Quarterly*, 23 (1970), 103-20.

———. "Hawthorne, Mary Ann, and 'The Lame Shall Enter First.'" *FOB*, 2 (1973), 3-18.

Grimshaw, James A., Jr. "The Mistaken Identity of Rufus [Florida] Johnson." *Notes on Modern American Literature*, 1 (1977), item 31.

Nelson, Ed. "Flannery O'Connor: A Religious Experience." *Columns* (Georgia College), Fall 1975, pp. 6-8.

"A LATE ENCOUNTER WITH THE ENEMY"

Tate, James O. "O'Connor's Confederate General: A Late Encounter." *FOB*, 8 (1979), 45-53.

"THE LIFE YOU SAVE MAY BE YOUR OWN"

Desmond, John F. "The Shifting of Mr. Shiftlet: Flannery O'Connor's 'The Life You Save May Be Your Own.'" *Mississippi Quarterly*, 28 (1975), 55-59.

Griffith, Albert J. "Flannery O'Connor's Salvation Road." *Studies in Short Fiction*, 3 (1966), 329-33.

Hegarty, Charles M., S.J. "A Man Though Not Yet a Whole One: Mr. Shiftlet's Genesis." *FOB*, 1 (1972), 24-38.

"PARKER'S BACK"

Browning, Preston, Jr. "'Parker's Back': Flannery O'Connor's Iconography of Salvation by Profanity." *Studies in Short Fiction*, 6 (1969), 525-35.

Fahey, William A. "Flannery O'Connor's 'Parker's Back.'" *Renascence*, 20 (1968), 162-64, 166.

Gordon, Caroline. "Heresey in Dixie." *Sewanee Review*, 76 (1968), 263-97.

"A STROKE OF GOOD FORTUNE"

Mayer, Charles W. "The Comic Spirit in 'A Stroke of Good Fortune.'" *Studies in Short Fiction*, 16 (1979), 70-74.

"A TEMPLE OF THE HOLY GHOST"

Mayer, David R. "Apologia for the Imagination: Flannery O'Connor's 'A Temple of the Holy Ghost.'" *Studies in Short Fiction*, 11 (1974), 147-52.
Walden, Daniel, and Jane Salvia. "Flannery O'Connor's Dragon: Vision in 'A Temple of the Holy Ghost.'" *Studies in American Fiction*, 4 (1976), 230-35.

"A VIEW OF THE WOODS"

Riso, Don, S.J. "Blood and Land in 'A View of the Woods.'" *New Orleans Review*, 1 (1969), 255-57.

"WHY DO THE HEATHEN RAGE?"

Burns, Stuart L. "How Wide Did 'The Heathen' Range?" *FOB*, 4 (1975), 25-41.

GENERAL CRITICISM

Browning Preston M., Jr. *Flannery O'Connor*. Crosscurrents Series. Carbondale: Southern Illinois University Press, 1974.
————. "Flannery O'Connor and the Demonic." *Modern Fiction Studies*, 19 (1973), 29-41.
————. "Flannery O'Connor's Devil Revisited." *Southern Humanities Review*, 10 (1976), 325-33.
Burns, Shannon. "Flannery O'Connor: The Work Ethic." *FOB*, 8 (1979), 54-67.
Burns, Stuart L. " 'Torn by the Lord's Eye': Flannery O'Connor's Use of Sun Imagery." *Twentieth Century Literature* , 13 (1967), 154-66.
Casper, Leonard. "The Unspeakable Peacock: Apocalypse in Flannery O'Connor." In *The Shaken Realist: Essays in Honor of Frederick J. Hoffman*. Edited by Melvin J. Friedman and John B. Vickery. Baton Rouge: Louisiana State University Press, 1970, pp. 287-99.
Coles, Robert. *Flannery O'Connor's South*. Baton Rouge: Louisiana State University Press, 1980.
Driskell, Leon V., and Joan T. Brittain. *The Eternal Crossroads: The Art of Flannery O'Connor*. Lexington: University Press of Kentucky, 1971.
Drake, Robert. "Flannery O'Connor and American Literature." *FOB*, 3 (1974), 1-22.
Eggenschwiler, David. *The Christian Humanism of Flannery O'Connor*. Detroit: Wayne State University Press, 1972.
Feeley, Sister Kathleen, S.S.N.D. *Flannery O'Connor: The Voice of the Peacock*. New Brunswick, NJ: Rutgers University Press, 1972.
Friedman, Melvin J., and Lewis A. Lawson, eds. *The Added Dimension: The Art and Mind of Flannery O'Connor*. New York: Fordham University Press, 1966.

Hendin, Josephine. *The World of Flannery O'Connor*. Bloomington: Indiana University Press, 1970.

Hines, Melissa. "Grotesque Conversions and Critical Piety." *FOB*, 6 (1977), 17-35.

Holman, C. Hugh. *The Roots of Southern Writing: Essays on the Literature of the American South*. Athens: University of Georgia Press, 1972, pp. 96-108, 177-86.

_____. *Windows on the World: Essays on American Social Fiction*. Knoxville: University of Tennessee Press, 1979, pp. 39-44.

Hyman, Stanley Edgar. *Flannery O'Connor*. University of Minnesota Pamphlets on American Writers, No. 54. Minneapolis: University of Minnesota Pamphlets 1966.

Ingram, Forrest L. "O'Connor's Seven-Story Cycle." *FOB*, 2 (1973), 19-28.

Ireland, Patrick J. "The Place of Flannery O'Connor in Our Two Literatures: The Southern and National Literary Traditions." *FOB*, 7 (1978), 47-63.

Katz, Claire. "Flannery O'Connor's Rage of Vision." *American Literature*, 46 (1974), 54-67.

Koon, William. " 'Hep Me Not To Be So Mean': Flannery O'Connor's Subjectivity." *Southern Review*, NS 15 (1979), 322-32.

Lackey, Allen. "Flannery O'Connor and Her Critics: A Survey and Evaluation of the Critical Response to the Fiction of Flannery O'Connor." M.A. University of Tennessee 1972.

Lensing, George. "De Chardin's Ideas in Flannery O'Connor." *Renascence*, 18 (1966), 171-75.

Martin, Carter W. *The True Country: Themes in the Fiction of Flannery O'Connor*. Nashville: Vanderbilt University Press, 1969.

May, John R., S.J. "Flannery O'Connor and the New Hermeneutic." *FOB*, 2 (1973), 29-42.

_____. *The Pruning Word: The Parables of Flannery O'Connor*. Notre Dame, IN: Notre Dame University Press, 1976.

McFarland, Dorothy T. *Flannery O'Connor*. Modern Literature Monographs. New York: Frederick Ungar, 1976.

Merton, Thomas. "Flannery O'Connor." *Jubilee*, November 1964, pp. 49-53.

Montgomery, Marion. "Flannery O'Connor, Eric Voegelin, and the Question That Lies Between Them." *Modern Age*, 22 (1978), 133-43.

_____. "Flannery O'Connor: Prophetic Poet." *FOB*, 3 (1974), 79-94.

_____. "The Prophetic Poet and the Loss of Middle Earth." *Georgia Review*, 33 (1979), 66-83.

_____. "Some Reflections on Miss O'Connor and The Dixie Limited." *FOB*, 5 (1976), 70-81.

Muller, Gilbert H. *Nightmares and Visions: Flannery O'Connor and the Catholic Grotesque*. Athens: University of Georgia Press, 1972.

Murphy, George D., and Caroline L. Cherry. "Flannery O'Connor and the Integration of Personality." *FOB*, 7 (1978), 85-100.

Nance, William L. "Flannery O'Connor: The Trouble with Being a Prophet." *University Review* (Kansas City, MO), 36 (1969), 101-8.

Neligan, Patrick, Jr., and Victor Nunez. "Flannery and the Film Makers." *FOB*, 5 (1976), 98-104.

Orvell, Miles. *Invisible Parade: The Fiction of Flannery O'Connor*. Philadelphia: Temple University Press, 1972.

Reiter, Robert E., ed. *Flannery O'Connor*. St. Louis: B. Herder Book Co., 1968.

Scouten, Kenneth. "The Mythological Dimensions of Five of Flannery O'Connor's Works." *FOB*, 2 (1973), 59-72.

Simpson, Lewis P. "The Southern Aesthetic of Memory." *Tulane Studies in English*, 23 (1978), 207-27.

Snow, Ollye T. "The Functional Gothic of Flannery O'Connor." *Southwest Review*, 50 (1965), 286-99.

Stephens, Martha. *The Question of Flannery O'Connor*. Baton Rouge: Louisiana State University Press, 1973.

Tate, James O. "The Uses of Banality." *FOB*, 4 (1975), 13-24.

Walters, Dorothy. *Flannery O'Connor*. Twayne United States Author's Series No. 216. New York: Twayne Publishers, Inc., 1973.

Wood, Ralph C. "The Heterodoxy of Flannery O'Connor's Book Reviews." *FOB*, 5 (1976), 3-29.

Wray, Virginia F. "Flannery O'Connor in the American Romance Tradition." *FOB*, 6 (1977), 83-98.

O'CONNOR AND OTHER AUTHORS

GRAHAM GREENE

Jacobsen, Josephine. "A Catholic Quartet." *Christian Scholar*, 47 (1964), 139-54.

NATHANIEL HAWTHORNE

Burns, Shannon. "The Literary Theory of Flannery O'Connor and Nathaniel Hawthorne." *FOB*, 7 (1978), 101-13.

Emerick, Ronald R. "Romance, Allegory, Vision: The Influences of Hawthorne on Flannery O'Connor." Ph.D. University of Pittsburgh 1975.

Montgomery, Marion. "The Artist as 'A Very Doubtful Jacob': A Reflection on Hawthorne and O'Connor." *Southern Quarterly*, 16 (1978), 95-103.

Walsh, Thomas F. "The Devils of Hawthorne and Flannery O'Connor." *Xavier University Studies*, 5 (1966), 117-22.

CARSON McCULLERS

Dorsey, James E. "Carson McCullers and Flannery O'Connor: A Checklist of Graduate Research." *Bulletin of Bibliography*, 32 (1975), 162-67.

Westling, Louise. "The Perils of Adolescence in Flannery O'Connor and Carson McCullers." *FOB*, 8 (1979), 88-98.

KATHERINE ANNE PORTER

Gretlund, Jan N. "Flannery O'Connor and Katherine Anne Porter." *FOB*, 8 (1979), 77-87.

NATHANIEL WEST

Cheney, Brainard. "Miss O'Connor Creates Unusual Humor Out of Ordinary Sin."
  Sewanee Review, 71 (1963), 644-52.
Hawkes, John. "Flannery O'Connor's Devil." *Sewanee Review*, 70 (1962), 395-407.
Zaidman, Laura M. "Varieties of Religious Experience in O'Connor and West."
  FOB, 7 (1978), 26-46.

CRITICISM BY SELECTED TOPIC

CHARACTERIZATION

Brittain, Joan T. "The Fictional Family of Flannery O'Connor." *Renascence*, 19
  (1966), 48-52.
Burns, Stuart L. "Freaks in a Circus Tent: Flannery O'Connor's Christ-Haunted
  Characters." *FOB*, 1 (1972), 3-23.
Flores-Del Prado, Wilma. "Flannery O'Connor's Gallery of Freaks." *St. Louis
  University Research Journal*, 2 (1971), 463-514.
Shear, Walter, "Flannery O'Connor . . . Character and Characterization." *Rena-
  scence*, 20 (1968), 140-46.

COMEDY

Sister Jeremy. "The Comic Ritual of Flannery O'Connor." *Catholic Library World*,
  39 (1967), 195-200.
Martin, Carter. "Comedy and Humor in Flannery O'Connor's Fiction." *FOB*,
  4 (1975), 1-12.

MANICHAEANISM

Carlson, Thomas M. "Flannery O'Connor: The Manichaean Dilemma." *Sewanee
  Review*, 77 (1969), 254-76.

PLACE

Cleary, Michael. "Environmental Influences in Flannery O'Connor's Fiction."
  FOB, 8 (1979), 20-34.
Desmond, John F. "Flannery O'Connor's Sense of Place." *Southern Humanities
  Review*, 10 (1976), 251-59.
Hoffman, Frederick J. "The Sense of Place." In *South: Modern Southern Literature
  in Its Cultural Setting*. Edited by Louis D. Rubin, Jr., and Robert D. Jacobs.
  1961; rpt. Westport, CT: Greenwood Press, 1974, pp. 60-75.
Spivey, Ted R. "Flannery's South: Don Quixote Rides Again." *FOB*, 1 (1972), 46-54.

VIOLENCE

Gossett, Louise Y. *Violence in Recent Southern Fiction*. Durham, NC: Duke University Press, 1965, pp. 75-97.

Rocco, Claire Joyce. "Flannery O'Connor and Joyce Carol Oates: Violence as Art." Ph.D. University of Illinois at Urbana-Champaign 1975.

Smith, J. Oates. "Ritual and Violence in Flannery O'Connor." *Thought*, 41 (1966), 545-60.

Index

ABOUT THE AUTHOR

James A. Grimshaw, Jr. is Professor of English and Director of the Department of English honors program at the United States Air Force Academy, Colorado. In 1977 he was Flannery O'Connor Visiting Professor of English at Georgia College, and in 1979-1980 he was Visiting Fellow in Bibliography at the Beinecke Rare Book and Manuscript Library, Yale University. He edited *Cleanth Brooks at the United States Air Force Academy* (1980) and is coauthor, with William E. McCarron, of *Persuasive Technical Writing* (John Wiley, 1981). He is author of *Robert Penn Warren: A Descriptive Bibliography, 1922-1979* (University Press of Virginia, 1981) and of articles and reviews in *Shakespeare Quarterly*, *Southern Review*, *Resources for American Literary Study*, and other scholarly publications.